Burn The Script

A Manifesto

Lisa Kirkman

About the Author

Lisa Kirkman knows what it means to live trapped inside a Script that was never hers. For decades, she followed the rules, played the roles, and checked every box that was supposed to lead to happiness. But deep down, she was dying inside, suffocated by expectations, fearful of the truth she had buried for too long. It took breaking everything she had built to finally step into the life she was meant to live.

Lisa is not just an author or a speaker, she is a truth-teller, a fire-starter, and a relentless advocate for radical self-ownership. She has walked the road from living inauthentically to standing fully in her truth, and now she is on a mission to help others do the same. She knows the fear, the doubt, the resistance that comes with burning the Script, but she also knows the freedom, the clarity, and the undeniable power that come on the other side.

With a background in coaching, storytelling, and personal transformation, Lisa has dedicated her life to guiding others through the fire, helping them unlearn the stories they have been told, dismantle the identities that no longer serve them, and build lives that are unapologetically their own. Through her writing, speaking, and coaching, she is here to remind you that you do not have to play by anyone else's rules. You do not have to shrink. You do not have to wait.

The time is now. The fire is burning. And Lisa Kirkman is here to help you light the match.

Dedication

*For my wife, Sharon, whose love and belief in me make
me braver than I really am. Without
you, this life would not have been possible.*
*For my friends, who have carried me through the turmoil,
with love, laughter, and doses of
reality. You are my anchor.*
*To Marilyn & Ruth, for showing me what it truly means to
be loved unconditionally by family.*
*And to anyone who has ever felt like they don't fit, this
book is for you.*

Author's Note

Before you dive in, I want to acknowledge something important.

This manifesto is a call to action, a challenge to step into your truth, to Burn the Script that was handed to you, and to reclaim your life. But I also know this:

For some, burning the Script is not just difficult, it is dangerous.

There are places in the world, cultures, and circumstances where stepping outside of expectations carries real consequences. For some, the cost of authenticity is rejection. For others, it can be far greater, threats to safety, security, or survival.

I am not naive enough to believe that freedom is as simple as deciding to change. That is a privilege not everyone has.

So, if you are reading this and thinking, *I want this, but I can't just walk away*, I see you.

This book is not an all-or-nothing demand. It is not a reckless push to destroy everything and start over. It is an invitation to move toward authenticity in whatever way is possible for you, safely, intentionally, and at your own pace.

For some, that might mean bold action, walking away, speaking out, setting fire to everything that no longer fits.

For others, it might mean small, quiet shifts, a private acknowledgment of truth, a boundary no one else sees, a gradual rewriting of internal narratives.

Even the smallest movement matters. A whispered truth. A decision made in secret. A single step forward, no matter how small.

Tiny movements, stacked over time, become revolutions.

So read this manifesto. Process it. Apply what you can in a way that keeps you safe. If your steps are smaller and your path is longer, it does not make your journey any less powerful.

You are not alone. And your freedom, however it unfolds, is still yours to claim. Your freedom is yours to define, there is no cookie cutter model for what freedom is.

Thank you for investing your time in yourself to grow and thank you for allowing me to be part of your journey.

With strength and solidarity,

Lisa Kirkman

Who Am I to Write This Book?

You might be wondering, who the hell am I to challenge the Script? To tell people to burn it all down and start fresh? For most of my life, I played my role perfectly. Country town girl, straight wife, business owner, ticking every box of what I was "supposed to" be. I convinced myself that if I followed the rules, I'd eventually feel like I belonged, like I was enough. Spoiler alert: I didn't.

At 46, I couldn't ignore the truth buried deep inside me anymore. I was gay. And that wasn't just a revelation about my sexuality, it was the cracking open of every single expectation, every "should," every lie I had lived by. Coming out wasn't just about admitting who I was to the world; it was about breaking free from the cage I'd built around myself, from a life scripted for me that I had never chosen.

I am not here to give you all the answers. I don't have them. I'm not some enlightened guru with a perfect, buttoned-up life or a foolproof system to fix whatever you're facing. If you're looking for a ten-step plan to guaranteed happiness, this isn't it. I am human, deeply human. Flawed, messy, still figuring things out. And I suspect you are too. We all carry stories, conditioning, and expectations we never consciously chose. Some of us have spent years following a Script that doesn't feel like ours, hoping that if we just check the right boxes, happiness and fulfillment will finally click into place. But what if the Script itself is the problem?

It was terrifying. It was messy. It shattered everything I thought I knew about myself. But in that destruction, I unlocked freedom, the kind of freedom you get when you stop pretending to be who everyone else wants you to be.

I rewrote my life, not in perfect little steps, but in big, ugly leaps of truth. Now, as a coach, writer, and host of the *Big Gay Overalls Podcast*, I help others find that same courage. I know what it's like to live a life that doesn't fit. I know the fear of stepping outside the lines. And I know the raw, undeniable freedom that comes when you stop hiding and finally choose yourself.

This book is not a quick fix. It's not a solution tied up in a neat little bow. But it is an invitation, a challenge to question, to unlearn, and to rewrite the rules you've been handed. The concepts I share here are powerful, not because they provide easy answers, but because they force you to think, to challenge, and to start laying the foundation for a life that is truly yours.

Burning the Script is not about chaos or reckless rebellion. It's about ownership. It's about finally allowing yourself to live in a way that aligns with who you truly are, not who you were told to be. It's about the journey of discovering who you actually are and making choices, not out of fear or for approval, but from a place of truth. This is your soul's journey, to come back home to yourself and abandon the expectations of the external world.

I won't pretend this work is easy. It isn't. It's uncomfortable. It's disruptive. It requires deep self-reflection and radical honesty. But I can tell you this: If you step into it, if you're willing to burn the Script and start writing your own, you will finally know what it means to be free.

So, if you're here because something inside you knows there has to be more, because you're tired of playing by rules that don't fit, you're in the right place.

Introduction: What is the Script?

The Script is the internal narrative you've been following, whether consciously or not. It's the set of beliefs, expectations, and rules that have shaped how you show up in the world. Maybe it was written for you by your upbringing, society, or past experiences. Maybe you've spent years playing a role that doesn't quite fit, editing yourself to meet unspoken expectations.

But here's the truth: the Script is not set in stone. You can rewrite it. You can step out of old patterns and choose a new, more authentic way of being. This journey is about recognizing where you are still performing, where you are still holding back, and making the decision to show up fully as yourself.

This is the work, the process of unlearning, reprogramming, and stepping into your truth. It's uncomfortable at times, but it's the only way to break free from a life that feels too small for who you are becoming.

The Fire That Must Be Lit

There comes a time when you can no longer ignore the truth staring back at you in the mirror. A moment when the weight of every expectation, every unwritten rule, every forced identity presses so hard against your chest that you can barely breathe.

You wake up to the reality that the life you are living is not your own. It was written for you, assigned to you, dictated by forces that never asked what you wanted, and forces you don't even know. And now, you stand at the edge of something terrifying and exhilarating: the realization that you do not have to follow the Script. But here's the truth, freedom will not be handed to you. No one is coming to grant you permission to live authentically.

You must unlock it.

You unlock it by walking through the abyss, by taking radical ownership, by stepping into the fire. You unlock it by rejecting the Script that was written for you and daring to write your own.

Burn the Script is not just a movement. It is not just an idea. It is a necessary revolution. It is the refusal to perform, to conform, to dilute our truth for the comfort of others. It is the declaration that we will no longer wait for freedom, we will claim it.

Why This Matters

Why does Burning the Script matter so much?

Because the price of staying inside the lines, of following the Script, is far greater than we realize. Sure, it's easy to think of the Script as just a set of rules about what we should do, how we should look, what we should aspire to. But these rules are more than just personal choices, they are the foundation of the systems we live in. These systems *shape* our lives, our relationships, our communities, and they control how we show up in the world. The longer we stay inside the Script, the longer we participate in a system that keeps us small, keeps us controlled, keeps us disconnected from each other and from our truest selves.

This isn't just about you. It's about all of us.

When you stay inside the Script, you're not just hurting yourself, you're perpetuating a culture of oppression, expectation, and conformity. Think about the times you've conformed to fit into someone else's ideal of who you should be. Maybe it was in your career, suppressing your voice and ideas because you feared stepping outside the accepted norms. Maybe it was in your relationships, bending to the pressure of what others expected from you, even at the expense of your own happiness. Maybe it was even in your body, forcing yourself to meet beauty standards that were never designed to reflect your truth.

But when we all do this, when we all live these small, controlled lives, playing our parts to fit the Script, we aren't just sacrificing our happiness. We're teaching others to do the same. We're reinforcing the idea that we are not allowed to be fully human, fully free. We reinforce the idea that we must be what society demands, what our families expect, and what our communities say we should be. We are taught to shrink ourselves, to apologize for our existence, to hide our truth. And when we hide our truth, we take away the space for others to do the same.

This is where the real cost lies. The consequence of living a scripted life doesn't just trap you, it traps the people around you. Your relationships, your friends, your children, they are all impacted by the way you live. If you stay small, if you stay confined by the Script, you are teaching those who look up to you that *this* is the way to live. That life is about following the rules, fitting into the mould, and giving up your authenticity for the sake of fitting in. What does that do to your family? To your friendships? To the future generation watching you?

And beyond that, your personal liberation is *linked* to collective liberation. The systems that keep us confined in these narrow expectations are the same systems that marginalize entire communities. It's the same Script that makes it harder for people of colour, for LGBTQ+ individuals, for women, for those with disabilities, for those in lower-income brackets, to live authentically. The societal Scripts are written to keep power in the hands of a few and to oppress those who don't fit the mould. Every time we conform, every time we choose to live within the lines, we reinforce those very systems of oppression. We say, "This is the way it's always been, and this is the way it will always be."

But here's the thing: *When you Burn the Script for yourself, you are lighting the way for others to do the same.* Your freedom to be yourself, truly, authentically, unapologetically, becomes a beacon. It shows others that they don't have to stay small, that they don't have to fit the mould, that they can burn their own Script too. The ripple effect is profound. When you step into your truth, you give permission to others to do the same.

And that's how we change the world.

Think about it: Every person who sheds the Script is not just reclaiming their individual freedom; they're dismantling the systems of control that have kept us all confined. They are challenging societal norms. They are breaking down the walls of oppression. They are saying *no* to the idea that we must all conform to the same standard. They are showing up for themselves, for their communities, and for the generations to come. And as more and more people Burn the Script, those systems begin to weaken. The walls start to crumble. The old, tired narratives start to shift. And before long, what was once the norm is no longer even a possibility.

This isn't just about personal empowerment; it's about collective liberation. When you choose to live authentically, when you choose to break free from the Script, you are changing the world, even in ways you can't always see. You are part of a larger movement, a force of change that is bigger than any one of us. And every time you make a choice that aligns with your truth, you are helping to create a more open, more compassionate, freer world for everyone.

This is why it matters. It matters because it's not just your freedom that's at stake; it's the freedom of everyone around you. It matters because the more we break free from the Scripts that confine us, the more we allow others to do the same. And in that freedom, we begin to create a world where we can all live authentically, together.

This is what we're fighting for. This is why we Burn the Script. Not just for ourselves, but for each other.

History will show us that Burning the Script is not new, it's been happening for centuries. It's an act that can change the world. Think about the suffragettes, who stood up against centuries of gender-based oppression and fought for the right to vote. They risked everything, faced ridicule and imprisonment, and yet their courage sparked a global movement that changed the course of history.

Think of the brave black students who broke the lines at college campuses during the Civil Rights Movement. They faced violent backlash, insults, and threats, but they knew that by challenging the Script of segregation, they were paving the way for a future where everyone had the opportunity to learn, to grow, and to live as equals. Their resistance to the cultural norms of the time wasn't just about their individual freedom, it was about creating a world where everyone could stand free.

The fall of the Berlin Wall marked a monumental moment in history when millions of people broke free from decades of political and social control. For years, the Script of oppression divided families, communities, and countries, but in 1989, the courage of those who refused to accept that division shattered the walls that had confined them.

Look at Nelson Mandela, who spent 27 years in prison, facing unimaginable hardship and suffering. But when he was released, he didn't just burn his own Script, he became the face of the movement that dismantled apartheid. Mandela didn't fight for his own freedom alone, he fought for the freedom of an entire nation, an entire people. His journey wasn't just about personal liberation; it was about the collective liberation of a country that had been bound by racial and social Scripts for centuries.

These moments in history show us the true power of breaking free. When we Burn the Script, we do more than reclaim our own lives, we ignite a fire that can break the chains of societal expectations for others. Every individual who has ever stood up, who has ever broken free from an oppressive Script, has made a difference that ripples out into the world. It's in those moments that true, lasting change happens. Your choice to Burn the Script is part of that legacy.

The Mission

To ignite a global movement of self-liberation, where people break free from inherited expectations, unlearn the silent rules that have kept them small, and build lives that are truly their own. Freedom is not a gift. It is a battle. It is unlocked.

Burn the Script is not about rebellion for rebellion's sake. It is about choosing authenticity over approval, freedom over familiarity, and truth over comfort. It is about refusing to live by default and instead, creating a life by design.

We are here to:

- Expose the invisible rules that dictate how we "should" live.
- Dismantle the conditioning that keeps people stuck.
- Teach people that freedom is something they must claim, through courage, action, and ownership.
- Build a community of self-liberators who refuse to settle.
- Replace fear-based living with radical self-ownership

The Vision

A world where:

- People are bold enough to live unscripted, choosing unlocked freedom over comfortable conformity.
- No one shrinks themselves to fit a role they never chose.

- Fear of judgment no longer dictates how people live their lives.
- Radical self-ownership, courage, and truth-telling become the standard.
- Every person has the clarity, confidence, and power to shape their own story.

Burning the Script is not just about personal liberation. It is about shifting culture. It is about undoing generations of inherited expectations, breaking cycles of waiting, of permission-seeking, of passive existence. It is about proving that there is another way.

The Just Cause

I am doing this because too many people are living lives that feel like slow deaths. There is nothing more tragic than spending decades playing a part you never auditioned for. I refuse to accept that this is just "how life is."

I fight for:

- Truth over tradition.
- Courage over compliance.
- Expansion over containment.
- Freedom over fear.

But understand this: Freedom is not given. It is unlocked.

You don't wish your way into an authentic life, you build it. You walk through the fire, you dismantle the old, and you write the new. With purpose, honesty, intention and grace. Grace for yourself but also others. The stories given to you weren't always done with malice, or ill intent. They were designed to keep you safe, to help you fit in. Because how many times were we taught that standing out was a bad thing? Black sheep of the family anyone?

This is not self-help. This is self-liberation. And it is not optional, it is necessary, if you truly want to live your most amazing life. Anything less than living your truth is a life half-lived.

So, if you are standing at the edge, wondering whether you have the strength to walk away from the Script you were given, let this be your answer: You do. You always have. But no one will hand it to you. You must claim it. You must step into the fire. You were never meant to follow. You were meant to create.

Burn the Script. Unlock your freedom. Reclaim your life.

Chapter 1: The Script We Were Given

The First Crack in the Script: The 'Never Enough' Cycle

"I never felt like I fit, not in my life, not in my skin. I followed the Script, checked every box, played the roles I was supposed to. And yet, I was always reaching for something else, the next job, the next level, the next 'cool' thing, hoping that maybe, this time, it would be the thing that made it all make sense."

"For a long time, that thing was workout shoes. I'd convince myself that a new pair, just the right pair, would finally be the one to make me feel whole. The hit would come the second I clicked 'buy,' a rush of dopamine, a fleeting illusion of excitement. And then, an hour later, the feeling was gone. The void was still there. So, I'd start searching for the next thing, then the next. It wasn't about the shoes. It was about the aching need to feel special, to feel like I mattered. To be seen."

"Yet, at the same time, I was terrified of actually being seen. I was stuck in this impossible space, I wanted to be someone, but I didn't even know who that was. I craved recognition, but I was hiding. I wanted meaning, but I was filling my life with things instead of truth. And I didn't understand, not yet, that the problem wasn't the job, the status, or the shoes. The problem was the Script I was following. A Script that never once asked me what I wanted."

What Is the Script?

From the moment we were born, we were handed a Script, a set of invisible, unspoken rules that dictate who we should be, what we should value, how we should behave, and what our lives should look like.

This Script is passed down through generations, reinforced by culture, family, education, religion, and society, shaping our beliefs, roles, and expectations without ever asking us what we truly want. It's the invisible checklist for what a "good person" does, how they live, and who they become. It tells us:

- Who we should love and how we should define relationships.
- What success looks like and what we must sacrifice to achieve it.
- How we should express our emotions, when to be strong, when to be quiet.
- Which roles we should play in our families, communities, and workplaces.
- How we behave.
- What we should aspire to look like.
- What we do.
- What we believe.

The Script relies on us simply absorbing the indoctrination and becoming blind followers who do not question. Because, in reality, we don't even know we can question it.

For example, in Western culture, the Script may teach a woman that she must prioritize being likable, nurturing, and accommodating, because stepping into her full power makes others uncomfortable. It may teach a man that vulnerability is weakness, that his worth is tied only to his productivity, that he must succeed at all costs. It may teach someone that their identity, love, or existence must fit into a narrow, predetermined box, or else they risk rejection, exile, or judgment.

The Introvert's Struggle

For many, the world operates on an extrovert's timetable. Loud conversations, crowded events, constant social interaction, these are seen as the "normal" ways to engage with the world. But for introverts, this constant push to "be seen" and "take up space" can feel overwhelming, draining, and completely out of alignment with who they are.

If you're an introvert, you've probably experienced the subtle (or not-so-subtle) pressure to modify your behaviour to fit into this extroverted world. You may have been taught to "speak up more" in meetings, "join the conversation" when you would rather observe, or "get out of your shell" when your idea of self-care is time alone with your thoughts. Society tells you that the quiet, reflective side of you needs to be fixed, as if your comfort in solitude is something to be ashamed of.

This isn't just about preferring a quiet evening at home over a party; it's about a deep, intrinsic need for space to process your thoughts, recharge, and connect with yourself. For introverts, these quiet moments are where clarity, creativity, and authenticity thrive. Yet, we live in a world that often values noise over substance, quantity over quality, and speed over thoughtfulness. Introverts are often forced to fight against their natural rhythm to match a more extroverted, faster-paced world.

The Script tells introverts that they must constantly project themselves outward, to be seen, heard, and acknowledged by others in ways that feel unnatural. This can lead introverts to internalize the idea that their quietness is a flaw, something that must be overcome to succeed, to belong, or to be "enough." The Script asks introverts to shrink their authenticity, just as it asks extroverts to tone down their natural exuberance.

But here's the truth: Introverts don't need to change who they are. In fact, the very thing that makes them introverted, deep thought, introspection, and a careful, measured approach to the world, are the qualities that allow them to live more authentically and intentionally. The Script doesn't honour these traits; it tries to mask them in favour of louder, more extroverted ideals. But introverts, by embracing their authentic selves, can rewrite the narrative. They can burn the Script and claim space for their inner world, without guilt or shame.

Why This Matters

Because too many people are suffocating inside a life that does not fit them. Because we have been conditioned to seek approval over authenticity, to prioritize predictability over passion, to measure our worth by how well we meet expectations that were set for us long before we had the chance to decide who we are.

We are taught to follow the rules, to play it safe, to fit the mould. Every area of our life is Scripted. We are given definitions of success, happiness, love, and identity, all crafted by someone else. We are taught that to belong, we must comply. That to be accepted, we must sacrifice pieces of ourselves. That to be loved, we must be smaller, quieter, easier to digest.

And so, we shrink. We fold ourselves into versions that are more palatable. We follow the Script. Until one day, we wake up and realize that in doing so, we have abandoned ourselves. We, in effect, disown parts of ourselves.

But what if we didn't? What if we stopped? What if we set fire to the Script and wrote our own story instead?

This Script was never written with our voices, our truths, or our desires in mind. It was crafted to make us fit, to keep us within the boundaries of what is safe, acceptable, and easy to control. The Script is not about you; it is about maintaining order.

It starts in childhood. The unspoken lessons shape us before we even have the words to challenge them. When you speak your truth as a child, you are told you are "too much." When you challenge authority, you are labelled "difficult." When you dream beyond the expected, you are warned to "be realistic." The Script is reinforced through school, family, media, religion, and culture until it is no longer a set of rules, it is a deeply ingrained belief that stepping outside these lines is dangerous.

At our earliest stages of development, it begins. Baby boys are treated roughly and as more resilient; baby girls are delicate and handled gently. They get different toys, different colours, everything is vastly different.

But here is the truth they never mentioned: The Script is not real. It is an illusion, a control mechanism, a cage disguised as certainty.

You were not put here to live a pre-approved life. You were not meant to follow someone else's blueprint. And yet, here you are, wondering why you feel restless, unfulfilled, and disconnected. It is because deep inside, you know this is not your story.

And that realization? That is the moment the fire starts. The moment you understand that you have been living a life that was never truly yours. You are faced with a choice: Do you continue playing the part, or do you Burn the Script and reclaim your life?

Chapter 2: The Scripts We Follow

From the moment we're born, we're handed a Script, a set of expectations, beliefs, and roles that shape how we live our lives. But these Scripts aren't one-size-fits-all. While many of us follow similar paths dictated by society, the Script is personalised, with variations that play out in different aspects of our lives.

The Many Faces of the Script

The Script isn't just a single story; it's a series of overlapping narratives that are shaped by the culture, society, and family we're born into. It's the set of rules handed down to us by those who came before, and it governs how we think, how we act, and who we believe we're supposed to become. But the truth is, the Script doesn't look the same for everyone. It's coloured by your culture, your background, your environment, and the systems that govern your life.

In the workplace, the Script is about achievement. It's about fitting into a specific mould, being the hardworking, high-achieving, ever-ambitious employee who sacrifices personal time for professional success. It's about climbing the ladder, fitting the corporate culture, and sacrificing personal authenticity for the sake of fitting in. The Script in the workplace rewards those who conform to the ideal image of professionalism, someone who doesn't make waves, someone who doesn't rock the boat. But this Script doesn't always serve us. It doesn't allow for individuality. It doesn't make room for different ways of working, different ways of being.

At home, the Script is about family expectations. The love and approval we seek from our families often come with conditions. For some, the Script says you need to become a doctor, marry young, have children, and live a life that follows a very specific timeline. But what happens when you don't want that life? When you want something different, something that feels truer to who you are, but you're scared of disappointing those who raised you? This Script doesn't always allow for that kind of freedom. It often demands that we choose between love and authenticity, making us feel like we can't have both.

And then there's the Script that's shaped by social media. It's the version of life that's filtered, curated, and edited for public consumption. On Instagram, Facebook, and TikTok, we're constantly bombarded with the idea that we need to look perfect, be happy all the time, and live a life of constant adventure. The Script here tells us that success is defined by likes, shares, and followers, and if you're not living up to the idealized version of yourself, you're not enough. It creates an unrealistic standard, one that's driven by comparison and external validation, and it's suffocating.

But the Script doesn't just affect us in personal spaces, it's deeply tied to the systems of power that govern our society. For those who are marginalized by race, class, gender, or ability, the Script becomes a much more complex and often painful reality. The Script for a man of colour, might be shaped by the systemic racism that dictates how he's perceived and treated by society. For a woman of colour, the Script could demand she fit into both the gender and cultural expectations, each one more restrictive than the last. And for someone in a lower-income background, the Script might tell them that their worth is tied to how much money they can make, how successful they can become within a system that was never designed to help them succeed.

The truth is that the Script doesn't treat everyone equally. It's shaped by privilege, by power, and by history. And for some, burning the Script means confronting not just personal expectations, but societal structures that have been in place for centuries. It means challenging the very systems that dictate who get to succeed and who gets to belong.

These variations of the Script exist because each of us is influenced by different forces, but they all share one thing in common: they limit us. They trap us in a life we didn't choose. In this manifesto, we'll explore how to burn these Scripts and liberate ourselves from their constraints, so we can live lives that are truly our own.

The Career Script

Alex sat at his desk, staring at the glowing screen in front of him. Another email notification popped up; another meeting scheduled for later that afternoon. He sighed, leaning back in his chair and running a hand through his hair. It had been years since he'd felt any spark of excitement in his job. He'd followed the path so many people told him was the right one, work hard, climb the corporate ladder, get the promotions, and the money would follow. But now, in his mid-thirties, after years of long hours, endless meetings, and countless business trips, Alex felt like he was suffocating.

He had the title. He had the salary. But none of it felt like success. He felt disconnected, disconnected from his work, from his values, from himself.

For so long, he'd been chasing the Script, the one society had handed him: climb, compete, succeed. But as he sat there in that sterile office, he realized he wasn't chasing his own dreams. He was just playing a part in someone else's story.

The realization hit him like a ton of bricks. *What if this isn't it? What if I've been chasing the wrong version of success this whole time?*

For weeks, Alex wrestled with that question. He thought back to the reasons he had originally chosen his career, his love for problem-solving, his drive to create meaningful change, his excitement about new ideas. But somewhere along the way, those sparks had dimmed. The long hours and the endless pursuit of more, the next promotion, the next pay raise, had drowned out the things that had once made his work feel meaningful.

One day, after another sleepless night of scrolling through job ads and thinking about making a change, Alex found himself at a crossroads. He could keep chasing the same Script, hoping that one day he'd feel fulfilled, or he could burn it all down and start rewriting his own path.

And so, Alex decided to Burn the Script. But like any change, it wasn't an easy decision. The first few steps were filled with doubt, uncertainty, and fear.

The moment he set a boundary, deciding that he wouldn't stay late anymore just because "that's what you do in this job", he felt the eyes of his colleagues on him. He could feel the judgment. "Alex doesn't care about this job anymore," they might have said. But the more he thought about it, the more he realized that he had been playing a role for far too long, working late, answering emails at all hours, all because it was expected of him. It wasn't serving him or his dreams. It was just part of the Script.

But giving up those late nights wasn't enough. Alex needed more. He started carving out time to work on something he'd always wanted to do, teach. For years, he'd dreamed of creating online courses for aspiring entrepreneurs; to share the knowledge he'd gained in his corporate career. But every time he'd start, he'd stop. "I don't have time," he'd tell himself. "I have to focus on my career first."

Now, as he burned the Script of what his career was supposed to look like, he made time. The first course was rough, but Alex poured his heart into it. It wasn't perfect, but it was his. It felt like he was finally doing something for himself, not for a boss or for some corporate ladder.

Still, the doubts came. *What if I fail? What if this doesn't work?* The fear that he wasn't making enough money from his side business, that it was all just a pipe dream, crept in. He found himself staring at his bank account, wondering if he should just stay in his stable job for another year or two.

But Alex didn't give in. Instead of letting fear take over, he used it. Every time he felt scared, he remembered the reason he'd started. He wasn't burning the Script to make more money or gain more status. He was doing it for his own freedom. For his own sense of fulfillment.

Slowly but surely, the more Alex focused on his side business, the more it grew. It wasn't an overnight success, but it didn't have to be. It was his. He began to feel the energy come back, not from a promotion or a bonus, but from doing work that was aligned with his values. He found peace in the small victories, watching his courses help people, getting positive feedback from students, and, most importantly, feeling like he was contributing something real to the world.

Eventually, Alex made the choice to leave his corporate job. It wasn't a grand, dramatic exit, it was a slow, intentional shift toward something more authentic. And for the first time in years, Alex felt truly successful. Not because of his job title, but because he had finally chosen to live a life that reflected who he really was, not who the Script told him to be.

And yes, it wasn't without setbacks. The doubts still came, especially when things didn't go as planned. But now, Alex had the tools to overcome them. He knew that burning the Script wasn't a one-time act; it was an ongoing process. Whenever he felt lost or uncertain, he reminded himself that it was okay to feel uncomfortable, that growth came from the discomfort. He also leaned on the strategies from this book: setting boundaries, embracing discomfort, practicing small steps, and, most importantly, knowing that failure was just part of the journey.

The Relationship Script

Sophia sat across from her partner, Michael, as they shared a quiet dinner at their favourite restaurant. The ambiance was perfect, the soft glow of the candlelight, the gentle hum of conversation around them, but something felt off. It wasn't the food or the setting; it was the tension in her chest, the familiar weight of a question she'd been avoiding for years.

Is this really what I want?

For most of her life, Sophia had followed the Script that was expected of her. Get into a relationship, fall in love, get married, have kids, and live the "happily ever after" that was promised. It was the narrative that had been handed to her by society, her family, and even her closest friends. As a child, she was told that one day, she would meet someone special and start the life she'd always dreamed of. And that dream, for so long, had revolved around the idea of *marriage*.

Sophia and Michael had been together for six years. On paper, they had it all: they were good together, they had a stable relationship, and they'd even discussed the next steps, buying a house, getting married, having children. But the closer they got to that next step, the more Sophia felt like a stranger to herself. She loved Michael, but there was a part of her that kept whispering, *I don't know if this is what I want.*

Her friends were getting engaged, her family was constantly asking when she and Michael would follow suit, and the pressure to fulfill the Script of the "ideal relationship" felt suffocating. The more Sophia ignored the voice inside her that asked if marriage was really what she wanted, the louder that voice grew. She couldn't help but feel like she was just *going through the motions*, playing the role, she thought she was supposed to play.

One night, after a heart-to-heart with a friend, Sophia realised something that shook her to the core: she had been living someone else's idea of happiness. Marriage, children, and the "traditional family" path were all ideas that had been planted in her mind, not by her heart. She didn't know if she even wanted to get married, *not right now, not with Michael, and maybe not at all*. The truth was, she wasn't sure if she ever would. But the fear of disappointing those around her, her parents, her friends, society, held her back from fully embracing that truth.

Sophia decided, in that moment, that she needed to burn the Script. Not just the relationship Script, but everything it represented. She needed to stop pretending that her path had to look like everyone else's. It was time to stop living out someone else's expectations and start living her truth.

The next day, she sat down with Michael and told him everything. The truth about her uncertainty. The weight she'd been carrying about the future. The doubts that had been simmering under the surface for so long. It wasn't an easy conversation, and it wasn't one she wanted to have, but she knew it had to happen.

Michael was understandably shocked, hurt even. They'd talked about their future so many times, and now it seemed like everything they'd planned was in jeopardy. But as Sophia spoke her truth, she felt a sense of relief wash over her, like she was finally giving herself permission to breathe. For the first time in years, she wasn't playing a role.

Over the weeks that followed, Sophia and Michael had difficult, emotional conversations. They both needed time to process everything. Sophia knew that burning the Script meant she had to be willing to face the fear of change, the fear of what her life might look like if it didn't follow the path everyone expected. She spent hours journaling, reflecting on her true desires, and letting go of the guilt she felt for wanting a different future. She also worked on setting boundaries with her family and friends, having honest conversations about her need to live life on her own terms, even if that meant disappointing them.

But the hardest part was still to come. As much as she loved Michael, as much as she knew their relationship was special, Sophia realized that continuing down the path they'd planned wasn't true to herself. After weeks of reflection, she made the difficult decision to end the relationship. It wasn't a decision made lightly, but it was a necessary one.

The decision left her heartbroken, but also incredibly empowered. For the first time in her life, she was choosing herself. She wasn't choosing the role of wife, daughter, or girlfriend, she was choosing *Sophia*.

Sophia's journey of burning the relationship Script wasn't easy, and the emotional toll was far from over. As she moved through the process, she was confronted with doubt and guilt. Her friends couldn't understand why she'd end a relationship that seemed so solid, her family questioned her decisions, and the world around her constantly reinforced the idea that she was supposed to settle down. She felt a deep sense of loneliness, especially when she saw friends getting married and starting families.

There were nights when she cried herself to sleep, unsure if she had made the right choice. The pressure to conform to the Script was relentless. *What if I'm making a huge mistake? What if this is just my fear talking?*

Sophia learned to practice radical honesty, both with herself and with others. The guilt of disappointing those around her was overwhelming at times, but she reminded herself that living authentically meant staying true to her own desires. When faced with moments of doubt, she'd revisit the journaling prompts she'd used throughout the process: *What do I really want? What am I afraid of losing?* Reconnecting with her true self allowed her to push through the external noise.

One of the most difficult aspects of burning the relationship Script was navigating the judgment from others. Sophia learned how to set clear boundaries with her family and friends, gently but firmly explaining that her decision was about her own growth, not a reflection of their values. This boundary-setting was a critical step in reclaiming her power and prioritizing her emotional health.

After ending the relationship, Sophia made time for self-care and reflection. She joined a support group for women navigating similar journeys, where she could share her story and listen to others. She focused on healing, rebuilding her sense of self, and reconnecting with her passions outside of a relationship. She reminded herself that she wasn't defined by her relationship status and that being alone wasn't a failure, it was an opportunity for self-discovery.

While Sophia had her moments of loneliness, she also leaned on a strong support system of friends who were supportive of her decision. She sought out mentors who had made similar decisions and could offer advice from a place of experience. This network of support reminded her that she wasn't alone in her journey and that she had the strength to move forward.

Months later, Sophia felt a sense of peace she hadn't felt in years. She had rewritten her relationship Script, not by abandoning love, but by choosing a love that was true to herself. She learned that being in a relationship wasn't about following the Script; it was about authenticity and mutual respect. As she moved forward, Sophia stayed open to the possibility of love, but she no longer felt the pressure to conform to the timeline and expectations set by others.

Sophia wasn't defined by her relationship status anymore. She was defined by her own choices, her own growth, and her unwavering commitment to living authentically. And for the first time in her life, she felt truly free.

The Body Image Script

Jamie stood in front of the full-length mirror, staring at her reflection. The woman in the glass wasn't the one she recognised anymore, not really. Her body had changed, she'd gained weight, lost weight, toned up, and then undone it all. But it wasn't just her body that had changed, it was her entire sense of self. The mirror had always been a measure of her worth, but today, it felt like a stranger staring back at her.

For years, Jamie's life had been ruled by the body image Script. She had spent endless hours in the gym, counting calories, obsessing over the number on the scale. It wasn't just about being healthy, it was about meeting an invisible, impossible standard of beauty. *Thin* was what she was supposed to be. *Perfect* was what she had to look like. From a young age, she had been taught that beauty was the gateway to love, success, and happiness. The more she focused on perfecting her body, the more she believed that when she finally achieved "perfection," everything else would fall into place.

But that day, as she stood there looking at herself, she felt exhausted, physically and emotionally. She had followed every diet trend, joined every workout program, and still, the reflection in the mirror never matched the ideal. The pursuit of perfection had left her feeling hollow, like something was missing, and no matter how hard she tried, she couldn't quite reach it.

She had everything, success at work, a circle of friends, a loving family, but there was an emptiness inside. She had spent so much of her life trying to fit into a mould, but the more she shrank herself, the further she felt from her true self.

Jamie's turning point came one evening after a casual conversation with a friend. They were sitting at a café, talking about their lives and the pressures they felt to look a certain way. Her friend shared that she had recently decided to stop dieting altogether. *"I'm done,"* she said. *"I just want to be healthy but not obsessed. I want to live my life, not waste it away chasing some impossible standard."*

That was when Jamie realized the truth she'd been avoiding for years. She didn't want to live her life measuring everything by her body, constantly striving for some arbitrary version of beauty. She had burned the Script in so many areas of her life, why was she still following it when it came to her body?

Jamie decided it was time to let go. She couldn't keep trying to shrink herself into someone she wasn't, just to please others, or some idealized version of herself. She wasn't just burning the Script; she was choosing to reclaim her body on her terms, to stop letting it define her worth.

It wasn't easy. The first few weeks felt like she was betraying everything she had worked for. Every time she let go of an old habit, like skipping meals to be "good" or working out obsessively to compensate for eating, she was confronted with guilt and shame. *What if I gain even more weight? What if I lose control?* The pressure was relentless, and it often felt like the world around her was still pushing the same beauty standards, no matter how hard she tried to break free.

The doubts came crashing in. The mirror, once a source of validation, now felt like a constant reminder of her old Script. When she saw a friend post an image of herself looking "perfect" on social media, Jamie felt a pang of insecurity. The old Script had a way of sneaking back in. There were times when she'd try on clothes and feel defeated because they didn't fit the way she wanted them to. She'd find herself comparing her body to others, feeling that familiar sense of failure.

But Jamie knew that this journey was about more than just her body, it was about shifting the very way she viewed herself. She began to realise that *healing* wasn't just about how she looked on the outside. It was about freeing herself from the chains of self-judgment, from the Script that had dictated her worth for so long. It was about choosing to nourish her body, not punish it.

One of the first things Jamie did was redefine what health meant to her. She stopped focusing on numbers, whether it was the number on the scale, the calories she consumed, or the number of reps she could do at the gym. Instead, she focused on how she felt. She started to listen to her body, practicing mindfulness and honouring her hunger. If she wanted pizza, she ate it, without guilt. If she felt tired, she rested. Slowly, she learned that health wasn't about perfection, it was about balance, self-care, and joy.

Whenever Jamie found herself slipping back into old habits, like counting calories or criticizing her body, she'd pause and ask herself, *"Is this mine to carry?"* She would remember the work she'd done to unlearn these scripts and make a conscious effort to reject them. Instead of berating herself for not fitting into a "perfect" image, she began to affirm her worth in other ways. She looked at her body and said, *I'm grateful for what it can do, not what it looks like.*

Jamie started to focus on what made her feel good on the inside, not just the outside. She dove into activities she had pushed aside in the past, reading, painting, and volunteering. She spent time with people who didn't care about her weight or her appearance, but about her spirit and energy. She also began to work on her mindset, practicing gratitude for her body and its strength. Over time, she realized that her value didn't come from fitting into a specific body shape; it came from who she was and how she showed up in the world.

Knowing that change would take time, Jamie reached out to others who were also trying to break free from the body image Script. She joined an online support group for women who were learning to embrace body positivity, where they shared their struggles, successes, and journeys. This community gave her the courage to keep going when she felt defeated. The support system reminded her that she wasn't alone, and that self-love was a lifelong journey, not a quick fix.

Months later, Jamie stood in front of the same mirror. She didn't look different, not dramatically anyway, but she felt different. For the first time in years, she felt at peace in her own skin. The scale no longer held the power to dictate her mood. Her body was hers, not a project to perfect, but a vessel to carry her through life, to be cared for and nurtured. Jamie had burned the Script that told her, that her worth was tied to her appearance, and in doing so, she had found a deeper connection to herself.

She no longer felt the need to fit into someone else's mould of beauty. Her self-worth was no longer dependent on the approval of others, or on society's impossible standards. She had finally reclaimed her body as her own, and with that freedom, she was ready to embrace all the beautiful, messy, and authentic parts of who she truly was.

The Financial Script

Carlos had always thought of himself as responsible, smart, hardworking, dependable. The kind of guy who did what was expected, who followed the rules, and kept his head down. For most of his life, he had subscribed to the idea that financial stability was the ultimate goal. As a young man, he'd watched his parents struggle with money, and he vowed to never let that happen to him. He worked his way up in a well-paying job, steadily saving, investing, and making sure he always had enough. By the time he hit his 40s, he was living in a suburban home with his wife and two kids, a nice car in the driveway, and a retirement fund that looked secure. From the outside, he had everything he was "supposed" to want.

But inside, Carlos felt a gnawing emptiness that he couldn't shake. Every day felt like the same routine: wake up, work, come home, sleep, repeat. His life was neatly compartmentalised, he was a good provider, a responsible father, a reliable employee, but it didn't feel like *his* life. It felt like something he was just going through, checking off boxes as he went along, living according to the financial Script that told him success was about earning more, saving more, and getting more.

The turning point came one evening when Carlos was sitting on the couch, his laptop open in front of him as he scrolled through his bank statements. He saw the numbers in black and white, he was financially secure, but the numbers didn't bring him joy. As his mind wandered, he realized that his entire existence had been shaped by an invisible force: the idea that financial security was the key to a happy life. But when he really examined it, he realized that all this security had come at a cost. He had sacrificed so much in the name of financial success, his health, his happiness, and his passions. He hadn't truly lived. He had been so focused on saving for the future, on ensuring that everything was stable and predictable, that he had forgotten what it felt like to actually *enjoy* life.

One day, he sat his wife down, nervously shifting in his seat as he told her how he felt. "I just… I don't want this anymore," he said quietly. "The job, the house, the car. It's like I'm living for some future I'm not even sure I want. What if there's more to life than just saving and working? What if I've been chasing the wrong dream?"

His wife, Sarah, looked at him with concern, but also something else, something that Carlos hadn't expected. It was understanding. She had always known Carlos was driven, always knew how much he cared about his family's financial well-being. But now, as she saw the exhaustion in his eyes, she realized that it wasn't just about money, it was about the life he wasn't living.

Over the next few weeks, Carlos wrestled with the decision. He couldn't deny that the Script, the one that told him to work hard, save hard, sacrifice today for a more secure tomorrow, had been drilled into him his whole life. *But at what cost?* he thought. He felt like he was constantly moving toward something he couldn't even define. It was like he was running a race but had no idea what the finish line looked like.

The fear was overwhelming. What would people think if he stepped off the predictable path? What if he failed? His family had always been proud of how responsible he was with money. What if they saw him as reckless? He was so afraid of making a mistake that he kept himself stuck, day after day, in a job that drained him, doing work that no longer felt meaningful. He was burning out, and the more he thought about it, the more he realized that the very thing that was supposed to protect him, his financial security, was the very thing that had made him feel trapped.

But as the days passed, Carlos came to a realization: *he didn't want to live in fear anymore*. He wanted to create a life that was about more than just numbers, more than just saving for a future he wasn't even sure he wanted. He wanted to take risks, to follow his passion, to start living for himself, not for the Script he'd been given. He didn't want to just provide for his family; he wanted to *be* with them, to experience life with them, not just from a distance.

So, he made a decision. He decided to cut back on his work hours, take a pay cut, and spend more time doing things that made him feel alive. He started exploring his creative side again, writing, painting, and working on projects that had always been sidelined by his career. It was terrifying, but each step felt like he was shedding a weight he'd carried for years.

Of course, it wasn't easy. There were moments when the fear crept back in, and the pressure to conform to the financial Script returned with full force. His colleagues questioned his decision to slow down at work. Some of his friends didn't understand why he wasn't pursuing bigger promotions. They would ask him, *"Why settle for less?"* But Carlos had already started to shift his mindset. He realized that happiness wasn't about more, it was about living in alignment with who he really was.

He began saying no to the overtime shifts, no to the extra responsibilities that didn't light him up. He stopped worrying about what his friends thought and focused on what he wanted to create for himself and his family. Slowly, he began to feel more connected to his work. Instead of feeling trapped in a cycle of ambition for the sake of ambition, he felt like he was building something with meaning. It wasn't about *getting* more, it was about finding joy in what he already had.

Carlos knew he couldn't change everything overnight, but he had taken the first step. By letting go of the Script that told him money and stability were the only things worth striving for, he started to build a life that felt true to who he was. A life that wasn't about numbers on a bank statement, but about experiences, growth, and passion. He had burned the financial Script, and in doing so, he had begun to rebuild a life that was his own.

The Cultural Expectations Script

Priya stood in front of her parents, her heart pounding in her chest as they stared back at her. They had just spent the past hour talking about their hopes for her future, the "ideal" future that had been carefully laid out for her since she was a little girl. They talked about finding a good, respectable husband from their community, settling down, raising children, and continuing the traditions they had followed for generations. Priya's mother, with her gentle smile, had asked her, *"When will you finally settle down? When will you bring a good man into this family? Your father and I want to see our daughter married before we get any older."*

Priya smiled weakly, nodding along, but inside, everything inside her felt like it was cracking open. The pressure was suffocating. She loved her parents, but they had never truly asked her what *she* wanted. They only wanted to see her fit into a mould they had built for her, a mould that had been handed down to them by their parents, and theirs before them.

She'd spent most of her life following the Script, the cultural Script that said she should become a dutiful daughter, marry within the community, have children, and fulfill her role in the family as the one who would continue the legacy. But something inside Priya had always resisted that Script. She didn't know if she ever wanted to get married, at least not the way they envisioned it. She didn't know if she wanted to become someone's wife and mother, fulfilling the role that had been passed down to her like an inheritance she never asked for.

Priya had known, deep down, that if she ever challenged the Script, it would mean disappointment. It would mean causing her family pain. The expectations were clear, *this is the life you will lead. This is who you will become.* She had spent so many years repressing her feelings, trying to fit into a life that wasn't hers, pretending that the idea of an arranged marriage, living within the bounds of her family's expectations, was something she could accept. But the truth was that with every passing year, the weight of that Script grew heavier.

Priya had always been the "good daughter," the one who did what was expected. She studied hard, got good grades, and made sure to meet every family obligation. She rarely spoke up when her parents set their sights on a potential match, and when they talked about her future, she nodded along and smiled, though a part of her inside was suffocating. She tried to suppress her discomfort, to tell herself that one day, she'd understand why things had to be this way. But that day never came.

One day, while taking a quiet walk in the park, Priya had an epiphany. The sun was low on the horizon, and the breeze was gentle, but in that moment, Priya saw her life more clearly than she ever had. The thought that had been building for years finally broke through the surface like a dam bursting open: *This isn't my life. This isn't my choice.* The Script that had been handed to her by her culture, by her family, was not hers to carry anymore. She didn't want the life they wanted for her; she wanted to choose her own path.

The realization was liberating but also terrifying. She didn't know how to break free. She didn't know what her family would think if she rejected the life they had planned for her. Would they understand? Would they disown her? Every time she thought about speaking up, about telling her parents that she didn't want to follow their Script, the fear crept in. *What would they say? What would the community think?* She knew that, in their eyes, she would be a failure if she didn't marry a man they approved of. She would be seen as selfish, ungrateful, and rebellious.

The first time she spoke to her parents about it, it was harder than she had ever imagined. She tried to keep her voice steady, but the words felt foreign coming out of her mouth. "I'm not sure I want to marry anyone at all," she said. Her father's face froze. Her mother's eyes filled with tears. They didn't understand. They couldn't understand. It wasn't just about rejecting a marriage; it was about rejecting an entire way of life, the way they had always lived, the way they had always known.

The conversation didn't go well. There were tears, hurt feelings, and accusations. They told her she was being ungrateful. They told her she was breaking their hearts. Priya felt as though she was betraying them, but at the same time, she knew she was finally speaking her truth. The guilt was overwhelming, and for days, she couldn't shake the feeling that she had done something wrong. She felt torn between the love she had for her parents and the love she had for herself.

But as time passed, Priya started to feel a sense of freedom. Every time she faced the judgment of her family or the whispers from her community, she reminded herself that her life was hers to live. She wasn't wrong for choosing a different path. She wasn't selfish for wanting to explore who she truly was outside of the roles everyone had assigned her. She started setting boundaries, gently but firmly telling her parents that she needed time to figure things out on her own. She made it clear that her life was not something they could control anymore.

As she continued to speak her truth, Priya began to find a deeper sense of self. She embraced the discomfort, knowing that growth comes from confronting the things that scare us most. She realized that burning the cultural Script wasn't about abandoning her family or her culture. It was about honouring her true self, even if it meant going against what others expected. She wasn't rejecting her heritage, she was claiming it on her own terms, no longer defined by what others had told her she should be.

In the end, Priya didn't marry. She didn't follow the path her parents had set for her. But she did something far more powerful, she chose her own path. And though her family struggled to accept her choices, over time, they began to see that she was still the same daughter they had always loved, just a little more free. And Priya, finally, felt like she was living her truth.

Where Do I Start?

Take this short quiz to uncover where you're most stuck and how to break free from the Script that's been holding you back.

Instructions:

- Answer each question honestly.
- Keep track of your answers (A, B, C, or D).
- Your most common letter will reveal where you need to Burn Your Script first.

Quiz Questions

1. When you wake up in the morning, your first thought is...

A) I have so much to do for everyone else.
B) I have to push through another day of something I don't love.
C) I hope I don't say or do the wrong thing today.
D) I feel guilty for not being more grateful for what I have.

2. When making decisions, you mostly worry about...

A) Disappointing or upsetting others.
B) Making the wrong choice and ruining my future.
C) Being judged or misunderstood.
D) Hurting people who have supported me.

3. If you had permission to do anything you wanted, you would...

A) Set stronger boundaries and take more time for myself.
B) Quit or change something major in my life.

C) Finally be honest about who I really am.
D) Stop feeling guilty for wanting more.

4. The biggest lie I've been told about life is...

A) That I should always put others first.
B) That success and stability will make me happy.
C) That I need to fit in to be accepted.
D) That wanting something different means I'm ungrateful.

5. When you imagine stepping into full authenticity, you feel...

A) Scared - what if people don't like it?
B) Overwhelmed - how would I even start?
C) Anxious - what if no one understands me?
D) Guilty - would I be letting people down?

6. You've been avoiding making a change because...

A) I don't want to upset or inconvenience others.
B) It feels too risky to step away from what I've built.
C) I don't even know who I really am without my Script.
D) I don't want to seem selfish or ungrateful.

7. Your inner voice tells you...

A) You should be doing more for others.
B) You're too deep in to change now.
C) You're not strong enough to handle rejection.
D) You don't deserve more than what you have.

8. When someone gives you a compliment, you…

A) Brush it off or downplay it.
B) Feel like a fraud - if only they knew the truth.
C) Worry they're just being nice.
D) Feel like I don't deserve it.

9. If you stay on this path for the next 5 years, you will…

A) Be exhausted from taking care of everyone but myself.
B) Feel even more trapped in a life that doesn't fit.
C) Keep hiding my real thoughts, feelings, or identity.
D) Resent the people I've been putting first.

10. If you had to take one bold step toward change today, you would…

A) Set a boundary and say "no" for once.
B) Make a big decision I've been avoiding.
C) Finally express my real feelings.
D) Let go of the guilt and allow myself to want more.

Results: Where You Need to Burn Your Script

Scoring:

- Mostly A's → The People-Pleasing Script
- Mostly B's → The Success Trap Script
- Mostly C's → The Hiding Script
- Mostly D's → The Guilt & Obligation Script

The People Pleasing Script

"I've spent my life making sure others are happy, even at the cost of my own needs."

Where You're Stuck:
You've been conditioned to prioritize others over yourself. Your choices are shaped by fear of disappointing people, even if it means sacrificing your own happiness.

First Steps to Burn This Script:

- **Say "No" this week** without explaining or apologizing.
- **Identify one need you've been neglecting** - then do something about it.

The Success Trap Script

"On paper, my life looks great, but I feel stuck in something I don't actually want."

Where You're Stuck:
You've followed a "successful" life path that society (or family) told you would bring happiness, but it's not aligned with who you really are.

First Steps to Burn This Script:

- **List the "shoulds" you've been living by** (career, relationship, lifestyle).
- **Imagine your ideal life** without fear, what would change?

The Hiding Script

"I've been suppressing my real thoughts, feelings, or identity because I fear being misunderstood."

Where You're Stuck:
You've been hiding parts of yourself to fit in, avoid conflict, or keep the peace, but it's costing you authenticity and connection.

First Steps to Burn This Script:

- **Write down one truth you've been avoiding saying out loud.**
- **Express your real opinion** in a low-risk setting.

The Guilt & Obligation Script

"I know what I want, but I feel guilty for wanting it."

Where You're Stuck:
You've internalized the belief that choosing yourself is selfish, so you stay stuck not because you don't know what you want, but because you feel bad for wanting it.

First Steps to Burn This Script:

- **Challenge your belief:** Is it really selfish to want happiness?
- **Set one guilt-free boundary this week.**

Chapter 3: What It Means to Burn the Script

The Firestarter Moment: Walking Into the Abyss

"I knew the life I was leading was killing me, slowly, quietly, in a way that didn't look like death but felt like it. My weight was out of control because I medicated with food. I felt hollow, detached, like I was moving through life without actually being in it. I used to wonder if I was some kind of sociopath, like the character Dexter, except without the killing people part, of course. I wasn't emotionally absent because I didn't care. I was absent because I was disappearing under the weight of pretending."

"I was bone tired all the time. If I wasn't working, I was sleeping. And now, looking back, I realize, sleep was an escape. You don't feel anything when you're asleep. No fear, no conflict, no truth creeping in at the edges. Just nothing. And that nothing felt safer than facing what I knew deep down: I was living a lie."

"The day I told my then-husband, I was gay, I felt like I was walking straight into an abyss. I was convinced the world would end, that I was about to set off an explosion that would leave nothing but wreckage. But I stepped forward anyway, because staying where I was? That was a slow death, and I had already been dying for years."

"And here's what no one tells you: even after making the leap, even after walking toward my truth, nothing magically got better overnight. I didn't wake up a size 8 model. I didn't suddenly have all the answers. The food, the exhaustion, the need to numb, those things didn't disappear. Because burning the Script isn't the end of the work. It's just the beginning. You still must rebuild. You

still must fight for alignment. You still have to unlock your freedom, step by step, choice by choice. The Script didn't just disappear, I had to unlearn it, piece by piece."

Burning the Script is not just an act of rebellion. It is an act of self-ownership.

It is the moment you realise:

- You do not have to be who they expected you to be.
- You do not have to follow the rules that were never meant for you.
- You do not have to earn your worth by playing a role that suffocates you.

Burning the Script can feel terrifying. It is standing at the edge of the known world and stepping off, not because you know exactly where you will land, but because staying where you are is no longer an option. It is admitting that everything you have built within the confines of the Script may need to crumble before something real can take its place.

It means questioning every assumption that has dictated your decisions. It means challenging the belief that security is more valuable than freedom. It means confronting the fear that without the Script, you might be lost. But here is what they never told you, the Script never kept you safe. It only kept you small.

Burning the Script means rejecting the story that keeps you contained, compliant, and silent. It is not about recklessness; it is about truth, and it is also about choice. It is about deciding, once and for all, that you would rather live a life of uncertainty on your own terms than a predictable existence that was designed for someone else.

When you Burn the Script, you are not just destroying something, you are creating something. You are replacing compliance with choice, obligation with authenticity, fear with expansion. You are stepping into the unknown, yes, but you are doing it with the full force of who you are, rather than the watered-down version they wanted you to be.

You have an innate knowing of what is right for you. You don't need to learn anything. You simply need to listen to yourself. Hear that quiet voice inside. You already have the universe's most powerful guidance system within you, you just have to listen.

So, ask yourself: What is the cost of keeping the Script? What is the cost of burning it? And then ask the only question that truly matters - what is the cost of never knowing who you could have been if you had chosen freedom over fear?

Chapter 4: What We Stand For

The Moment I Knew My Script Wasn't Mine

"For most of my life, I followed a Script I didn't write. I ticked every box I thought I was supposed to. I got married. I built a life that looked like success from the outside. I played the role I was handed, convincing myself that if I did everything "right," happiness would follow.

And yet, inside, I was dying.

I remember the moment when the weight of it all nearly broke me. I was sitting in my car, gripping the steering wheel, unable to move. The truth was clawing its way out of me, a truth I had spent years silencing: I was gay.

Not in a theoretical, distant way. Not in a maybe one day I'll deal with this kind of way. I was living a lie. And every day I stayed in that Script, I was choosing to suffocate a little more.

But the thought of stepping into the unknown, of disrupting everything, of potentially losing people, of rebuilding my life from scratch, was terrifying. The weight of expectation, of what I had built, of what I thought I would lose, felt unbearable.

And so I sat there, in my car, staring at a choice that no one could make for me.

Do I keep following the Script? Or do I set it on fire and finally start living?"

Burn the Script is not just an idea. It is a revolution against everything that has tried to control you. It is the breaking of chains, the refusal to conform, the conscious decision to stop being a character in someone else's narrative and take full authorship of your own life.

It is about burning the illusion that you must shrink, fit in, or mould yourself into something palatable for others. It is about stepping into the fire of discomfort and walking out as the truest, most unfiltered version of yourself.

But let me tell you this, Burning the Script is not easy. It is not a single moment of awakening; it is a fight. It is a series of choices, small and massive, that test your courage over and over again.

Burning the Script is a Commitment

The truth? Burning the Script is not a one-time event, it is a commitment. It is choosing - over and over again - to step into truth, even when it terrifies you. It is deciding that you will no longer silence yourself to make others comfortable. It is waking up every day and refusing to retreat into the safety of the familiar, even when the unfamiliar feels impossible.

What We Believe

Your life does not need permission. No one but you can decide what is right for you. You are not here to follow rules that make you disappear. Your existence is not meant to be hidden, dulled, or tamed. You do not owe the world a version of yourself that makes them comfortable. The people who demand that you fit into their expectations are not your people.

Playing small serves no one. Shrinking to avoid judgment only ensures that you live a life dictated by fear. There is no right time to start living. The perfect moment will never arrive. The only time is NOW. Burning the Script is a declaration that you will no longer live for approval, tradition, or fear of rejection. It is a commitment to expansion, authenticity, and truth. It is a call to stand fully in your power, unapologetic and unafraid.

Are You Ready?

I will not lie to you; this will not be easy.

You will have moments where you second-guess yourself. You will have people who don't understand, who resist, who try to pull you back into the Script. You will have days when the fire of transformation feels too hot, too overwhelming, too much.

And yet, freedom is always worth it. I do not promise that this journey will be painless. But I promise you this: Nothing is more painful than living a life that is not your own. So, I ask you: Are you ready to Burn the Script?

Chapter 5: The Cost of Staying in the Script

The Moment I Realized I Was Dying Inside

"I used to think I could live both lives. That I could keep following the Script while carrying the weight of who I really was in secret. That as long as I was doing all the things I was supposed to, working hard, building a career, being a good wife, keeping everything together, then maybe I wouldn't have to feel the truth clawing at me from the inside.

But the cost of pretending is high.

I remember a night when it hit me like a freight train. I was sitting on the couch in my own home, watching TV. A totally ordinary night. But something about that moment cracked me open.

I felt like I wasn't even there. Like I had become a ghost in my own life.

Everything about my world looked "right" on paper. But inside, I was suffocating. It felt like a slow death, like I was fading into the background of my own story, becoming smaller and smaller until there would be nothing left of me at all.

And in that moment, I had a terrifying thought:

What if I just stayed like this? What if this was it? What if I woke up in ten years and I was still sitting on this couch, playing the role, watching my real life slip further and further away?

The fear of staying, of never living as my full self, became bigger than the fear of leaving.

That was the moment I knew: I could not keep paying this price."

Every Day You Stay in the Script, You Lose:

Another day of your life waiting to feel "ready."
(Newsflash: Ready never comes. If you wait for certainty, you will die waiting.)

Another moment of self-expression sacrificed for approval.
(How much of yourself have you already given away just to make others comfortable?)

Another year spent playing a role that was never yours.
(What would your life look like if you weren't living for someone else's expectations?)

The True Cost of Staying in the Script

Staying in the Script doesn't just cost you time, it costs you yourself. It erodes your confidence, replacing it with a life that is predictable but passionless. It forces you into spaces where you feel unseen, unheard, and unfulfilled. It teaches you to be so afraid of rocking the boat that you become the one drowning.

The longer you follow the Script, the harder it becomes to recognize your own voice beneath the noise of expectations. And one day, you will wake up and wonder how you got here.

You will look back at the moments where you silenced yourself. Where you said yes when you wanted to say no. Where you buried parts of yourself to make others more comfortable.

And you will ask:

- What if I had burned it sooner?
- What if I had been brave enough to choose my own path, no matter how uncomfortable, how uncertain, how disruptive?
- What if I had never let fear write my story?

Because here's the truth: The cost of staying in the Script is not just a life of compromise. It is a life unlived. And that is a price too high to pay.

The Choice You Must Make

So now, you must decide: Do you keep paying the price, or do you set yourself free? Do you choose to keep shrinking, or do you step into your truth, fully, fiercely, unapologetically? Do you keep waiting for permission, or do you claim your life as your own?

There is no "right" time. There is no guarantee it will be easy. But there is one guarantee that matters: If you keep following the Script, you will never be free. And if you don't take your life back now, when will you?

Chapter 6: This Is Your Turning Point

The Moment I Knew

"I didn't know it was a turning point at the time. I just knew I couldn't keep living like that.

For years, I had convinced myself that if I followed the Script, if I did everything I was supposed to do, checked every box, played the part well enough, then eventually, I would feel whole. I would feel at peace. I would feel something.

But I didn't.

Instead, I felt like I was disappearing. Like every time I silenced a truth, it chipped away at me. Every time I smiled through discomfort, swallowed my needs, played it safe, I lost another piece of myself.

And then one day, I couldn't ignore it anymore.

It wasn't a dramatic, earth-shattering moment. It wasn't a lightning bolt of realization. It was quieter than that, just a deep, undeniable knowing. A whisper that had grown into a roar.

This is not my life. This is not who I am supposed to be.

And once I let myself see that truth, there was no going back.

That was my turning point."

There comes a moment when you know. When you feel it deep in your bones that you cannot keep living like this.

The weight of the Script you have been carrying, of expectations, of rules you never agreed to, of a life that does not feel like your own, has become unbearable. And in that moment, a fire ignites. A reckoning begins.

This is your turning point. This is where you decide whether to stay within the lines that have kept you contained or step into the unknown and claim your life for yourself.

For some, the turning point comes suddenly, like a lightning strike, an event, a realisation, a betrayal, a loss that shakes everything loose. For others, it is a slow unravelling, a quiet awareness growing louder and louder until it can no longer be ignored. No matter how it comes, it is here now. And you must choose.

Do you keep following the Script, hoping it will eventually lead you to happiness, fulfillment, freedom? Or do you burn it and step into the raw, unpredictable, but undeniably real life that is waiting for you?

The Fear of Leaving the Script

Walking away from the Script can feel terrifying. It means shedding layers of identity that once felt safe, abandoning beliefs that have shaped your decisions, and facing the unknown with nothing but your own intuition to guide you. It is losing approval from those who benefitted from your conformity. It is confronting the question: *Who am I, if not who I was told to be?*

But the fear of staying is greater. Because to stay is to betray yourself. To stay is to choose comfort over truth, predictability over authenticity, and survival over actual living. To stay is to accept that your life will never truly be yours.

And so, you reach the edge. The moment of decision. You can either step back into the life you know, the one that feels safe but suffocating, or you can take the leap and set yourself free.

The Leap into the Unknown

Burning the Script does not mean you have all the answers. It does not mean you will suddenly know exactly what to do next, consciously at least. But it means you are choosing yourself. It means you are trusting that you are capable of creating something real, something meaningful, something true.

It will not be easy. The voices of doubt will try to drag you back. The world will tell you to be careful, to reconsider, to not ruin what you have. But what they do not understand is that what you have is not yours. It is borrowed. It is Scripted. And you are done living someone else's story.

The Decision to Burn the Script

This is the moment where you reclaim your life. The moment you stop waiting. The moment you stop seeking permission.

No one is coming to save you. No one is going to rewrite the Script for you. No one is going to hand you the life you were meant to live. You must take it. Be your own hero. You must burn the old story and start writing your own.

So, ask yourself: Are you ready? Are you done waiting for the perfect time, the perfect plan, the perfect version of yourself? If you are, the fire is already burning. All you have to do is let it consume everything that was never truly you.

I know what it feels like to stand at the edge of change, staring into the unknown, terrified of what happens if you take that step. I know how tempting it is to stay where it's familiar, even if it's suffocating. But I also know this: Nothing is scarier than the thought of waking up ten years from now, still trapped in a life that doesn't belong to you.

If you're feeling it now, that pull, that unrest, that knowing, it's not a mistake. It's not a phase. It's not something to ignore. It's your truth, trying to set you free.

And at some point, you will have to decide: Do I keep betraying myself, or do I finally choose me? This is your turning point. Choose yourself. Choose freedom. Burn the Script.

Chapter 7: The Burn the Script Oath

The Weight Lifting: True Freedom

"And then, one day, I realized, I felt lighter. The world hadn't ended. The abyss I feared? I had stepped into it and found solid ground. I no longer needed permission. I wasn't waiting to be accepted, I already was. The weight I carried for decades had burned away, and for the first time, I knew what real freedom felt like."

"I didn't fully recognize the change in myself until someone else pointed it out. A friend messaged me after seeing one of my posts and said, 'Your smile is different now, it reaches your eyes. It's coming from within.' And I knew exactly what they meant. For so long, I had mastered the performance of happiness. I knew how to smile in a way that looked right. But before, no matter how hard I tried, my eyes gave me away. There was always a sadness there, an emptiness I couldn't fully hide. But now? Now, it was real. Now, I felt the happiness radiating from the inside out, because for the first time, I wasn't living for someone else's expectations. I was living for me."

Burning the Script is not just a moment; it is a commitment. It is a declaration that you will no longer live under someone else's expectations, nor will you wait for permission to be fully yourself. It is the promise you make to yourself that from this day forward, you will walk your own path, no matter how uncertain, no matter how unconventional, no matter how much resistance you face.

You do not Burn the Script once and walk away. You burn it every time you refuse to shrink to fit. You burn it every time you choose your truth over approval. You burn it every time you stand in your power and say, "I am done living a life that was not mine."

If you choose to Burn the Script, you are choosing:

- Radical self-ownership over external validation.
- Truth over comfort.
- Authenticity over approval.
- Action over waiting.
- Freedom over fear.

The Fire Will Test You

There will be moments when you doubt yourself. When the old voices creep in, whispering that maybe the Script was safer. When the world makes you feel reckless for walking away. When you wonder if you should have stayed where it was predictable, where you knew what was coming next.

But safety is an illusion. The Script never protected you; it only numbed you. It kept you caged in expectations, living a half-life dictated by someone else's standards. Burning the Script means choosing risk over regret, choosing to feel fully alive instead of just existing.

The Oath of the Unscripted Life

Say this out loud or write it down where you can see it every day. This is your oath. This is your contract with yourself:

"I will no longer live by rules I did not create.
I will no longer shape myself to be more digestible for others.
I will no longer wait for someone else to tell me I am enough.

I will own my choices. I will own my voice. I will own my life.
The past does not define me. The Script does not control me.
From this moment forward, I choose myself."

Burning the Script is not the end of the story. It is the beginning of something new, creative, dynamic, powerful, something unscripted, something that is yours. The question is no longer, *What happens if I leave the Script?* The question is now, *What will I create in its place?*

The fire is still burning. No more waiting. No more asking. No more Scripts.

Who are you without the Script? It is time to find out.

Chapter 8: How To Start the Fire

You've seen the Script for what it is, a set of rules, expectations, and obligations that were handed to you, not chosen by you. You've questioned its grip on your life. You've begun to understand how it shaped your decisions, your relationships, your self-worth.

Now, it's time to do something about it.

Burning the Script isn't just a thought exercise. It's an action. It's a rebellion. It's a conscious decision to stop living by a narrative that was never yours and start creating a life that actually fits. But fire doesn't start on its own. It needs friction. It needs fuel. It needs air to breathe.

This section is about striking the match. It's about the how, the tangible, practical steps that will take you from knowing you need to change to actually doing it. Because insight without action is just another way of staying stuck.

Here, you will learn how to:

- Set boundaries and reclaim your time so you stop living at the mercy of others.
- Redefine success on your terms so you no longer chase empty achievements.
- Rewrite your core beliefs so you stop seeing yourself through the lens of outdated expectations.
- Take bold, unapologetic action to start living in alignment with your truth.

This is the part where your life begins to shift - not just in your mind, but in reality. The fire is waiting. Let's start it.

Why Boundaries Are the Foundation of Freedom

You've burned the Script. You've started questioning the rules you were given. But here's what no one tells you: If you don't protect your time, your energy, and your truth, the old Script will creep back in.

Ask yourself:

- Who in my life expects me to be available at all times?
- Where do I say "yes" out of obligation, not desire?
- What activities drain me, but I keep doing them because I'm afraid of disappointing people?
- Who gets access to my time, emotions, or energy without earning it?

If you feel exhausted, resentful, or stuck, it's not because you're doing too much. It's because you're doing too much for everyone else, and not enough for yourself. Boundaries are what keep your truth intact. They are not about pushing people away. They are about holding your ground so that the real you can finally breathe.

Decide What You're No Longer Available For

Most of us have been taught that setting boundaries is selfish. That saying "no" is rude. That good people don't disappoint others. That is a lie.

The truth:

- Setting boundaries doesn't push the right people away. It filters out the wrong ones.
- Saying "no" doesn't mean you don't care, it means you care about yourself, too.

- If someone gets angry because you have a boundary, that's proof that the boundary is needed.

Exercise: The "HELL NO" List

Write down everything you are done tolerating, emotional labour, toxic conversations, unrealistic expectations.

Examples:

- I am no longer available for last-minute favours that disrupt my day.
- I am no longer available for guilt-tripping conversations.
- I am no longer available for energy-draining friendships.
- I am no longer available for people who only reach out when they need something.
- I am no longer available for unpaid emotional labour.

Pick one thing from your list. Commit to enforcing it this week.

The Art of Saying No (Without Guilt or Over-Explaining)

"No" is a full sentence. If that makes you uncomfortable, you probably need this section the most.

Boundary Scripts That Work:

When someone asks for your time:

- "I can't commit to that right now."
- "I don't have the capacity for that."

- "I have other priorities that need my focus."

When someone pushes past your boundary:

- "I hear you, but my answer is still no."
- "I know this is disappointing, but I need to honour my limits."
- "I've made my decision."

A boundary is a limit, not a discussion. You don't need permission to set it.

Key Rule:
No over-explaining. No apologizing. No justifying.

Enforcing Boundaries Without Fear

You can set all the boundaries you want, but if you don't enforce them, they don't exist.

What to Expect When You Set Boundaries:

- Some people will respect you more.
- Some people will test you.
- Some people will throw a tantrum.

Let them*. That is not your problem. That is their adjustment to your new self-respect.

If someone gets upset because you won't meet their demands, that is proof that the boundary was needed.

Action Step: The next time someone pushes your boundary, repeat it without caving.

Example:

- **Them:** "Can you just do this one little thing for me?"
- **You:** "I can't. That doesn't work for me."
- **Them:** "Oh, come on, it'll just take a minute."
- **You:** "I understand, but my answer is still no."

*Mel Robbins, *The Let Them Theory: The Life-Changing Mindset That Makes It Easy to Say No, Set Boundaries, and Free Yourself from the Stress of Other People's Expectations* (HarperCollins, 2024).

Reclaiming Your Time Like a Boss

Your time is the most valuable resource you have. If you don't protect it, someone else will take it.

Three Non-Negotiables for Reclaiming Your Time:

1. **Schedule Time for Yourself FIRST.**
   Don't wait until after you've helped everyone else. Put your needs on the calendar first.
2. **Stop Justifying Your Free Time.**
   You don't need an excuse to say no. Rest is a valid reason.
3. **Create an Exit Strategy.**
   Have a go-to phrase for removing yourself from draining conversations, events, or commitments.

Example Exit Lines:

- "I have to go, but let's catch up another time."
- "I'm not available for that."
- "I need to prioritize something else right now."

Pick one of these exit lines and use it this week.

24 Hour Boundary Challenge: Take One Bold Step

Let's put this into practice - starting now.

Your 24-Hour Challenge:

- Set one clear boundary today.
- Say "no" to something you don't want to do (without apologizing).
- Protect one hour of your time for yourself, guilt-free.

Reflection: How did it feel? What happened when you enforced your boundary?

Boundaries Are the Key to Burning the Script

If you want to reclaim your life, you must start by reclaiming your time.

You are NOT responsible for:

- Other people's reactions to your boundaries.
- Making everyone comfortable at your own expense.
- Saying "yes" to things that don't align with you.

This is your life. If you don't protect it, no one else will.

Redefining Success

For most of your life, success has been defined for you. It was the degree, the job, the marriage, the house, the title, the bank balance. It was productivity, respectability, and meeting expectations.

It was a Script.

And maybe you've achieved parts of it. Maybe you checked all the right boxes. But if success was supposed to feel fulfilling, why does it feel like something is missing?

The truth is: Success, as you were taught, was never designed to fit you. It was designed to control you. It's time to break that definition apart and rebuild one that actually fits.

Step 1: Identifying the Inherited Version of Success

To redefine success, you must first see the version you've been living by.

Ask Yourself:

1. Growing up, what was I told "success" looked like?
2. Who in my life reinforced this version of success?
3. Have I ever achieved a goal that was supposed to make me happy, but left me feeling empty?
4. Whose definition of success am I still trying to live up to?

Many of us are chasing an outdated version of success because it was handed to us by parents, teachers, religion, culture, or society. But the reality is, success that is externally defined will never feel like true success.

Step 2: Breaking the Old Definition

If the success you were handed doesn't fit you, it's time to let it go.

Exercise: Success Myth-Busting

Write down the definition of success you've been following.

Example:

- *Success means having a stable, high-paying job.*
- *Success means being married with kids.*
- *Success means being productive all the time.*

Now, for each statement, challenge it.

- *Who told me this was true?*
- *Do I actually believe this, or was I conditioned to believe it?*
- *What if I could redefine success completely? What would change?*
-

Step 3: Creating Your Personal Definition of Success

If you could wipe the slate clean, what would success actually mean to you?

Ask Yourself:

- What makes me feel most alive, even if it doesn't fit society's definition of success?
- What do I deeply value that has nothing to do with money, status, or achievement?

- If I could be successful in a way that looked completely different from my past expectations, what would that look like?

Success might not be about working harder. It might be about having more time for yourself. Success might not be about proving your worth to others. It might be about learning to believe in your worth, regardless of external validation. Success might not be about what you achieve. It might be about how deeply you experience life.

Step 4: Writing Your New Success Manifesto

Now that you've broken the old definition, it's time to create your own personal Success Manifesto.

Exercise: Define Success in Your Own Words

Complete these sentences:

Examples:

Success, to me, is no longer about constantly proving my worth through productivity.
Success, to me, is about feeling free, at peace, and in alignment with my values.
I will know I am successful when I wake up excited about my day, not just surviving
through it.
The kind of life I want to build is one where I prioritize joy, creativity, and deep relationships over external achievements.

Success, to me, is no longer about

_____

_____

Success, to me, is about

_____

_____

I will know I am successful when

_____

_____

The kind of life I want to build is

_____

_____

Step 5: Living Your Redefined Success

Defining success is one thing. Living by it is another.

This means:

- Saying no to opportunities that look "impressive" but don't align with your values.
- Prioritizing things that bring you fulfilment, even if they don't make sense to others.
- Measuring success based on how you feel, not how you look to the outside world.

You don't need to explain your new definition to anyone. You just need to start living it.

The Freedom of Defining Success for Yourself

Success is not about how others see you. It's about how you see yourself when you wake up in the morning. Success is not about what you accumulate. It's about how much of your life feels like yours.

Success is not about impressing people who wouldn't trade lives with you anyway. It's about creating a life that feels deeply fulfilling, even if it looks completely different from what you once imagined. This is your definition now. Live by it.

Rewriting Your Core Beliefs

"The most powerful prison is the one you don't realize you're in."

The Unseen Chains of Your Core Beliefs

You were given a Script. It taught you who you should be, how you should act, what you should strive for. It shaped your fears, your decisions, your sense of self-worth. But what holds that Script in place?

Not the people who wrote it. Not society. Not even external rules.

It's your **core beliefs**, the invisible, unquestioned rules that dictate how you see yourself and the world.

- *"I have to work hard to be worthy."*
- *"If I say no, people will stop loving me."*
- *"Being different means being alone."*
- *"Success is about proving myself to others."*

These beliefs are not truths. They are just stories you have been told so many times that they feel like reality. And as long as you live by them, the Script remains intact.

If you want to burn the Script, you must go deeper. You must rewrite the beliefs that hold it together.

Step 1: Identify the Beliefs That Are Holding You Back

Most of us don't consciously choose our core beliefs. They are absorbed from childhood, shaped by culture, reinforced by experiences. To rewrite your beliefs, you must first see them clearly.

Ask Yourself:

- What beliefs do I have about myself that feel limiting or heavy?
- Where did these beliefs come from? (Parents, teachers, society, past experiences?)
- How have these beliefs shaped my decisions and behaviours?
- Have I ever questioned if they are actually true?

Exercise: The Belief Audit

Write down three beliefs you've carried most of your life.

Now, challenge each one:

- *Where did I learn this?*
- *Is this always true, or is it just something I was told?*
- *Who benefits from me believing this?*
- *What would change if I no longer believed this?*

Example:

Belief: *"I have to achieve in order to be valuable."*

- Where did I learn this? → From parents who only praised me when I accomplished something.

- Is this always true? → No. I have worth even when I'm not being productive.
- Who benefits from this? → Work cultures, society, people who exploit my need to prove myself.
- What would change if I stopped believing this? → I could rest without guilt. I could create without pressure. I could finally feel enough.

Step 2: Dismantle the Old Beliefs

A belief is just a thought you've repeated so many times that it feels like truth. If you want to change it, you must interrupt the pattern.

Rewriting Exercise: Replace the Lie with a New Truth

Take each limiting belief and rewrite it into a statement that aligns with the life you want.

Examples:

Old Belief → New Truth

- *"If I say no, people won't love me." → "The right people will respect my boundaries."*
- *"I am only valuable when I'm productive." → "My worth is not tied to what I achieve."*
- *"Being different means being alone." → "Being fully myself attracts the right people into my life."*
- *"I have to earn rest." → "Rest is my right, not a reward."*

Write your new belief in the present tense, as if it's already true. Your brain doesn't respond to what is "possible", it responds to what is declared.

Step 3: Live the New Beliefs Before You Fully Believe Them

This is where most people get stuck. They think they must fully believe their new truth before they can act on it. But belief follows action, not the other way around. If you start living as if your new beliefs are true, your brain will catch up.

Challenge: Act As If

Pick one rewritten belief and test it in real life.

Example:

- New Belief: *"I don't have to explain myself when I say no."*

  - Action: Say no today without justifying it.

- New Belief: *"I am enough, even when I'm not achieving."*

  - Action: Take a full day off without guilt.

You are proving to yourself, through action, that the new belief is real.

Step 4: Rewrite Your Personal Truth Statement

Now that you've broken the old beliefs and begun living by new ones, it's time to define your own truth. Write a personal statement that reflects your new way of seeing yourself and the world.

Example Truth Statement:

- *I do not exist to meet other people's expectations.*
- *I do not have to earn my worth—it is already mine.*
- *I trust myself over anyone else's opinion of me.*
- *I give myself permission to change, to grow, and to choose my own path.*

Read this every morning. Make it part of you. This is your new foundation. You are the author now. Your core beliefs have shaped your life up until this moment. But they do not have to shape your future. You get to decide what is true for you.

Burn the old stories. Write new ones that make you feel free.

TAKE BOLD, UNAPOLOGETIC ACTION

"You don't think your way into a new life. You act your way into it."

The Difference Between Wanting Change and Creating It

By now, you've burned the Script. You've questioned your beliefs. You've redefined success. You've set boundaries. And yet, none of that matters if you don't act. There is a moment when every revolution moves from theory to reality. From internal shifts to external changes. From thought to movement. This is that moment for you. Thinking about change is not enough. Reading about freedom is not enough. You must step into it. You have to take bold, unapologetic action.

Step 1: The Myth of Waiting Until You're Ready

Most people never take action because they're waiting for the right moment.

> *"I'll start when I'm more confident."*
> *"I'll do it when I have more time."*
> *"I just need to prepare a little more."*

These are all lies we tell ourselves. Yes, even me too.

Confidence comes from action, not before it. Clarity comes from movement, not planning. The right moment will never come. You must create it. If you wait to be ready, you will be waiting for the rest of your life.

Step 2: Identify Your "Burn the Bridge" Move

If you want to guarantee you won't go back to the old Script, you must burn the bridge to it.

Ask Yourself:

- What have I been avoiding because it feels too big, too scary, too uncertain?
- What action would make it impossible for me to go back to the life I don't want?
- If I weren't afraid of failing, what would I do today?

This is your burn-the-bridge move. The action that makes the old life impossible to return to.

Examples:

- **If you want to quit your soul-sucking job:** Submit your resignation today.
- **If you're tired of hiding who you are:** Tell the truth to one person right now.
- **If you've been stuck in indecision:** Pick the choice that scares you most, and go all in.

This isn't about recklessness. It's about commitment. When you remove the option of turning back, the only way is forward.

Tony Robbins often references the **"Burn the Boats"** philosophy, a concept rooted in historical accounts of leaders who, upon arriving at enemy shores, ordered their men to **burn their boats**, eliminating any possibility of retreat.

The message is clear: when there's no way back, the only option is to move forward and win. Robbins uses this as a metaphor for commitment, when you remove your escape routes, when you stop keeping one foot in your old life "just in case," you force yourself to fully commit to the path ahead.

This isn't about recklessness; it's about decisive, all-in action. When you burn the boats, you eliminate hesitation, fear-driven backpedalling, and half-hearted effort. You signal to yourself, and the world, that you are done entertaining the old ways and fully stepping into the life you are creating.

If you're serious about burning the Script, you can't leave a safety net for your past. The only way to make real change is to make retreat impossible.

Step 3: Move Faster Than Your Fear

Fear is not the problem. The problem is giving fear too much time to talk you out of action. Fear thrives in hesitation. It grows in the space between your decision and your action. If you want to break through, you must move before fear has a chance to stop you.

The 5-Second Rule for Bold Action:

Mel Robbins, in her book The 5 Second Rule, explains that hesitation is the death of action. The moment you feel the urge to do something, whether it's speaking up, making a bold decision, or stepping into an opportunity, you must physically act within five seconds.

Otherwise, your mind will start rationalising, creating excuses, and keeping you stuck. Robbins developed this method as a way to override fear and build confidence through immediate action.

This principle directly applies to burning the Script, if you wait until you "feel ready," you'll never take the leap. The only way forward is to act before fear stops you.

- The moment you decide to do something, count down from five and act before you reach zero.
- Do not give yourself time to analyse or justify.
- Just do it.

Examples:

- You want to send that email? **5-4-3-2-1 - SEND.**
- You want to have that hard conversation? **5-4-3-2-1 - CALL.**
- You want to post that vulnerable truth? **5-4-3-2-1 - PUBLISH.**

When fear knows it only has five seconds to stop you, it loses its power.

Step 4: Make Discomfort Your New Normal

You've spent your whole life trying to stay comfortable, stay safe, stay in line. But nothing grows in comfort. No revolution happens without discomfort. If you want a new life, you must be willing to sit in the discomfort of breaking the old one.

New Rules for Unapologetic Action:

- If it scares you, it's probably the right move.
- If it feels too big, break it into smaller steps, but take the first one NOW.

- If other people don't like it, it's a sign you're finally making decisions for yourself.
- If it feels uncomfortable, good, that means you're expanding.

Step 5: Prove to Yourself That You Are This Person Now

Bold action isn't something you do once. It's a way of being.

Your Challenge:

Take one action today that the old version of you would never have taken.

Examples:

- Say what you actually mean, instead of what's expected.
- Walk away from something that doesn't serve you, without explaining why.
- Make the investment in yourself that you've been scared to make.
- Make a decision without overanalysing it.
- Show up fully in your truth, even if it makes people uncomfortable.

Once you do it, you will realize:

This is who you are now. You are not the person waiting to be brave. You are not the person stuck in indecision. You are not the person following the Script. You are the person who moves. Who chooses. Who acts. And once you see yourself this way, you can never go back.

You Either Act, or You Don't

At the end of the day, there is no in-between. You either take the leap, or you don't. You either say yes to yourself, or you keep waiting. You either live boldly, unapologetically, or you stay small. The fire is already burning. Step into it.

Chapter 9: How to Use This Manifesto

This manifesto is not just something to read, it is something to live. It is not a book to put down and forget. It is a call to action. A challenge. A demand that you step into the person you were always meant to be.

But freedom is not a passive state. It is not something that simply happens to you. You must unlock it. This work requires action. It requires choices. It requires stepping into discomfort, again and again, until your authentic life becomes your only way of being.

Here's how you begin:

1. Read It, Again and Again

Burning the Script is not a single act. It is a process. A daily practice. There will be moments when doubt creeps in, when fear whispers that maybe you should go back, when the world tries to convince you that you were safer in the Script.

Read this manifesto in those moments. Let it anchor you. Let it remind you that freedom is not about feeling safe, it is about stepping into your power.

Action Step: Set a reminder in your phone once a week to revisit a section of this manifesto. Reflect on where you are in your journey. What part of the Script is still pulling you back? What fire do you need to walk through next?

2. Identify the Scripts That Are Holding You Back

You cannot burn what you have not named. The Script you've been following didn't just appear overnight, it was handed to you in pieces, layered over time. Some of it came from family. Some from culture. Some from the quiet rules no one spoke aloud, but you still learned to obey.

Action Step: Write down the rules you've been living by that no longer serve you. What silent expectations have shaped your decisions? What beliefs have kept you playing small? Be brutally honest. Then ask yourself: Who would I be without these?

3. Speak Your Truth, Even When It Shakes You

Burning the Script is not just an internal process, it is something you must live out loud. That means using your voice, even when it feels uncomfortable. It means telling the truth, not just to yourself, but to the world.

Freedom is unlocked in the moments when you choose to show up fully, without apology. It is in the hard conversations, in the boundaries you enforce, in the times you refuse to shrink to make others comfortable.

Identify one place in your life where you are still editing yourself, at work, in relationships, or in the way you speak about your dreams. This week, take one step toward full honesty. Say the thing. Set the boundary. Show up as the person you are becoming. The discomfort will pass, but the power of owning your truth will stay with you.

4. Share It with Those Who Need It

There are people in your life who are suffocating under their own Scripts. People who feel trapped but do not yet have the words for it. People who are waiting, just like you once were.

Be the catalyst for their awakening. Let them know they are not alone.

Action Step: Share this manifesto with one person who needs it. Have a conversation about it. Ask them: What's the Script you've been living by? What would it look like for you to burn it? Liberation spreads when we light the fire for others.

5. Take One Bold Action Toward Freedom

You do not think your way into freedom. You act your way into it. This is not about grand gestures or overnight transformations. It is about the daily decision to choose yourself. To live in alignment with who you are, instead of who you were told to be.

Action Step: Every morning, ask yourself:

What is one thing I can do today that moves me closer to my unscripted life?

Then do it. Every single day.

6. Embody It Every Day

Your life should be the proof that burning the Script is possible. Every decision you make, every truth you speak, every way you show up should be a testament to the fact that you refuse to live a Scripted life.

This is not about rebellion for rebellion's sake. This is about building something real, a life that is fully, completely, unapologetically yours.

Action Step: Commit to one visible shift that reflects your unscripted life. Change something about your space, your routine, your appearance, anything that makes you feel like you are stepping into the person you were always meant to be.

7. Listening to Your Inner Knowing

Deep inside, there's a voice that knows the truth. A knowing that doesn't need logic or approval. It's raw, real, and relentless. It whispers when we ignore it, screams when we betray it, and settles when we finally listen.

But how do you hear it? How do you trust it?

How to Listen to Your Inner Knowing

1. **Notice the Discomfort**
   Your inner knowing isn't always a loud declaration; it often starts as discomfort. That tension in your gut when you say "yes" but mean "no," the exhaustion after forcing yourself into spaces that don't fit, the subtle resentment when you do what's expected instead of what's right for you. Discomfort isn't failure; it's feedback.

2. **Question the 'Shoulds'**
   Any time you catch yourself thinking, *I should do this*, stop and ask: *Who says?* Is this something you truly want, or just a rule you've absorbed? Your knowing isn't buried under noise, it's buried

under Scripts written for someone else's comfort.

3. **Get Quiet and Get Honest**
   Sit with yourself. Breathe. Ask, *What do I really want?* Then, listen. The answer isn't always immediate or convenient, but it's there. It might show up as a feeling, a pull, an undeniable truth you've been avoiding. Give it space.

4. **Trust Your Body's Signals**
   When something is right for you, your body responds. There's ease, expansion, energy. When something is wrong, there's tightness, fatigue, a deep sense of resistance. Learn the difference between fear (which can signal growth) and misalignment (which signals self-betrayal).

5. **Act on It**
   Inner knowing is useless if you ignore it. The more you listen, the stronger it gets. The more you act, the more aligned you become. Start small. Say no when you mean no. Walk away from what drains you. Move toward what lights you up.

How It Feels When You Don't Listen

- Like you're constantly holding your breath.
- Like you're wearing a mask that's getting heavier.
- Like you're playing a role in someone else's play.
- Like you're shrinking, numbing, avoiding.
- Like you're waiting for permission to be yourself.
- Like you're an imposter, fraud or character in a story.

Ignoring your inner knowing isn't just uncomfortable, it's unsustainable. The longer you suppress it, the louder it fights back. Anxiety, burnout, restlessness, resentment, these aren't personal failures. They're alarms, warnings that you're off track.

Practical Guidance on How to Begin

Burning the Script is a huge, transformative step, but it can feel overwhelming when you're standing at the edge of it, unsure where to start. You might be reading this and thinking, *I'm stuck. I know I need to make a change, but where do I even begin?* The good news is it doesn't require one big dramatic leap. It starts with small, intentional steps, steps that help you see where the Script is at play in your life and give you the courage to start breaking it down.

So, where do you begin?

The First Step

The first step is about awareness. You can't burn a Script you don't recognize. It's time to take a good, honest look at where you're still following someone else's plan for your life. Start by asking yourself a few simple, yet powerful questions:

- Where in my life do I feel stuck or unfulfilled?
- What parts of my life do I feel pressured to live up to?
- Are there areas where I'm doing what's expected, rather than what I truly want?

This process doesn't need to be done in one sitting. Don't rush it. Take time to reflect and jot down your answers. Start with the big-picture aspects (career, relationships, health) and work your way down into smaller, more specific areas (daily habits, social media habits, work routines).

The Micro-Scripts

You may think of the Script as one big, overarching narrative, but often, it's made up of smaller scripts, the "micro-Scripts", that are easier to identify and begin deconstructing. These micro-Scripts are often subtle and ingrained in daily life, and they can be harder to spot because they feel normal. These are the habits, expectations, and roles that quietly run your life. They might include:

- **Work Habits:** Do you feel pressured to answer emails after hours? Are you stuck in a cycle of overworking, just to prove you're valuable?
- **Family Roles:** Are you living out an expectation of what a "good daughter/son" should be? Are you constantly putting family obligations before your own needs?
- **Social Media Persona:** Do you find yourself curating your life online in ways that don't align with who you truly are? Are you posting to get validation rather than sharing your authentic self?

These micro-Scripts are often easier to tackle first because they feel more manageable. Once you start noticing them, you'll have a clearer path forward. Start small. Begin with one micro-Script that feels particularly restrictive. Ask yourself:

- How am I showing up in this area that doesn't align with who I am?
- What would it look like to show up differently, to be authentic in this space?

This could mean turning off notifications after a certain time so you're not enslaved by work emails, or it could mean showing up online without the curated version of yourself, letting go of the pressure to perform for likes and followers.

Taking Action: Small, Intentional Shifts

Once you've identified the micro-Scripts, the next step is to take intentional, small actions to break them. The goal here is not to completely overhaul your life in one go, but to start making small shifts that bring you closer to the life you want to live.

Here's how you can begin:

- **Create Space for Yourself:** If family expectations are running your life, set a boundary. It might feel uncomfortable at first, but it's an essential step toward reclaiming your space. Start by saying no to something you don't want to do. It could be as simple as declining an invitation or setting a limit on how much time you spend on certain family obligations.
- **Reclaim Your Time:** If work habits are keeping you from your personal life, start by setting new boundaries. Maybe it's turning off your email notifications during weekends or designating certain hours as "non-work" hours. The key is to protect your time so that you can devote it to things that align with your true self.
- **Shift Your Online Presence:** If social media feels like a curated performance of who you're supposed to be, take a break from posting for validation. Start by sharing something real and raw, or even just something that represents your true self. It doesn't have to be perfect. In fact, it shouldn't be. Reclaiming your online presence as

an authentic space is one of the most powerful small steps you can take.

Small Wins Lead to Big Change

Rebuilding your life after burning the Script doesn't need to be overwhelming. It's about recognizing the micro-Scripts and taking one small step at a time to shift them. Consistency is key. The small changes you make now will build on each other, creating a stronger foundation for your authentic life.

And remember, it's okay to start small. Every tiny shift in the right direction is a victory. You're not going to solve everything all at once, and you don't need to. The magic lies in the steady, consistent effort to align your life with your true self.

Don't Rush the Process

This is a journey, not a sprint. Don't expect overnight transformation. Give yourself permission to take small, imperfect steps. You'll face setbacks. There will be moments when the Script feels familiar, and it will pull you back in. But this process is about progress, not perfection. Celebrate the small wins, acknowledge the setbacks without judgment, and keep moving forward at your own pace.

The first step is awareness. The second is action. And the third is compassion for yourself throughout this journey. Keep reminding yourself that this is a lifelong process, and you're allowed to take it at the pace that feels right for you.

Chapter 10: The Long-Term Process of Rebuilding

You've burned the Script. The fire is out, and now you're standing in the ashes. The initial burst of freedom and relief may have passed, and now you find yourself facing a new reality, a reality where you're not just shedding the old, but actively creating the new. This is where the real work begins. The process of rebuilding is where transformation happens, and it's not a one-time event. It's a slow, steady process of becoming who you were always meant to be.

The first thing you'll notice is the emptiness. You've burned away the old identity, and for a while, it will feel like a void. But that's okay. It's in the void that the new version of you can take shape. And while the void can feel uncomfortable, it's also full of potential. Every choice you make now is a step toward reclaiming your true self. The beauty of rebuilding is that it doesn't happen overnight. It happens in small, everyday actions. It happens in the way you choose to live your life, one decision at a time.

There will be setbacks, no doubt. Doubts will creep in. Old habits will resurface. You'll wonder if you've made the right choice. You'll second-guess yourself. But that's part of the process. Transformation isn't linear. It's a winding road, full of ups and downs. The key is to keep going, even when it feels hard. When you hit a setback, take a breath, regroup, and keep moving forward. This is where the real strength is built, not in the moments of certainty, but in the moments of doubt.

You don't have to do it alone. Support is essential in the rebuilding process. Surround yourself with people who understand your journey and who encourage you to keep going. Seek out mentors who have walked this path before and find communities that support the authenticity you're striving for. These people will be the mirrors you need to reflect your progress and remind you that you're on the right path.

This process isn't about perfection, it's about consistency. Some days will be easier than others. Some days, you'll feel completely in sync with your authentic self. Other days, you'll feel lost, like you're not making any progress. But it's all part of the journey. The small, daily steps you take to stay true to yourself will eventually add up, and the work you put in now will pay off over time.

Rebuilding is a lifelong process. It's about evolution, becoming more of who you really are, every single day. Your journey isn't finished. It's just beginning. And the more you align with your core values, the more you'll see the world shift around you, as your authentic self begins to take centre stage.

Chapter 11: Rest, Healing, and Rebuilding

The act of burning the Script is undeniably powerful, a fierce, liberating moment when you choose to break free from the expectations that have bound you. But after the fire is out, after the smoke clears, it's important to acknowledge that there's more to this journey than simply destruction. Burning the Script is the beginning of your transformation, but it's also a process of emotional and mental recalibration. It's a delicate time, and it's normal to feel both empowered and exhausted, a contradiction that can be difficult to navigate. So, how do you find balance after the fire? How do you give yourself the rest and healing necessary to rebuild, refuel, and reclaim your centre?

Why Healing Matters

When you burn the Script, you're not just discarding a set of societal expectations, you're confronting the very parts of yourself that have been shaped by those expectations for most of your life. This isn't a simple or easy process. It's not just about shifting career paths, setting new boundaries in relationships, or changing your lifestyle. It's about releasing years, sometimes decades, of conditioning. It's about undoing everything you thought was "supposed" to make you happy. And that kind of emotional and mental work can leave you feeling drained.

After the fire, you may experience emotional exhaustion, mental fatigue, or even identity confusion. You might wonder, *Who am I now?* and *How do I rebuild from here?* You've gone through a process of shedding your old skin, but now it's time to allow yourself space to heal and replenish. This healing is just as vital as the burning itself, because without it, you'll find it difficult to sustain the energy needed for your ongoing journey.

Rest: The Essential Act of Replenishment

Rest is not a luxury; it's a necessity for growth and rebuilding. When we think of burning the Script, we often focus on the dramatic change, the release, the act of destruction. But change also requires space to breathe, time to recalibrate, and energy to nurture. Rest allows us to process the emotions that come with shedding the old and finding the new.

Take the time to pause. Let yourself rest, physically, mentally, and emotionally. You don't have to be in constant motion after burning the Script. There's no race to "get it right" or to "become" someone new immediately. In fact, moving too quickly after such a significant life change can be overwhelming and counterproductive. So, give yourself permission to take time off, time to simply exist without the pressure of constantly moving toward the next thing.

One way to embrace rest is by creating quiet moments in your day, time when you don't have to "do" anything but simply be. This could mean setting aside a few minutes in the morning or evening for mindfulness or meditation or simply enjoying a cup of tea without checking your phone or worrying about your to-do list. These moments of rest will help you process everything that has shifted and allow your mind and body to catch up with the emotional work you're doing.

Healing Practices for Emotional Restoration

While rest is essential, healing requires more than just physical relaxation, it demands emotional care. After burning the Script, you're likely to feel a mix of exhilaration and grief. You've just let go of a major part of your identity, and that's bound to create space for complex emotions. This is when you need to tend to your inner world.

Journaling is a powerful practice to help you process your thoughts and emotions. Writing allows you to reflect on your journey and helps you make sense of the chaos. Spend some time each day (or week) writing about how you're feeling. What has changed? What emotions are surfacing? What do you need to release and what do you want to invite into your life? Don't censor yourself, let the words flow freely.

Another important practice is meditation or breathwork. These techniques help calm the nervous system, allowing you to centre yourself and release tension. As you meditate or practice deep breathing, focus on letting go of any remaining fears or self-doubt. Affirm to yourself that you are worthy of this change, that the pain of shedding the old will be worth the beauty of becoming your true self. Meditation can be a grounding force, giving you clarity and peace in moments of uncertainty.

You might also consider connecting with nature. Nature has an incredible ability to heal, and spending time outside can help you feel reconnected to the earth, to yourself, and to the present moment. A walk in the park, a hike in the mountains, or simply sitting outside and breathing deeply can help you gain perspective, release negative energy, and realign your focus.

Finally, don't underestimate the power of self-compassion. After burning the Script, there will be moments when you feel lost or adrift. In those times, remind yourself that this journey is not about perfection, it's about progress. You are allowed to feel vulnerable. You are allowed to grieve the parts of yourself you've let go of. And most importantly, you are allowed to be gentle with yourself as you rebuild.

Restoring Your Energy

Once you've given yourself the rest and emotional healing you need, the next step is to restore your energy. When you're rebuilding your life after burning the Script, it's easy to feel drained, but the energy you're seeking to rebuild isn't just about physical rest, it's about reconnecting with your passions.

Spend time doing things that bring you joy, things that reignite your inner spark. Maybe it's painting, cooking, traveling, or simply spending time with the people who make you feel alive. These activities help you rediscover who you are outside of the Script, allowing you to reconnect with what fuels you. The more you feed your soul with activities that resonate with your authentic self, the more your energy will return.

And remember, this isn't a race. You don't need to rush your healing. Let the process unfold naturally. It's important to give yourself the permission to heal and the space to rest, especially after such a significant transformation.

Why This Matters

Healing and rest are not just necessary for personal wellbeing, they are essential for the continued journey of self-liberation. You cannot build a sustainable, authentic life if you're running on empty. Healing allows you to recharge, to realign with your deepest desires, and to find the inner strength required to move forward.

Without rest and healing, the process of transformation can become overwhelming. The emotional toll of shedding your old life requires time, compassion, and understanding. The act of burning the Script is powerful, but it's just one part of a lifelong journey. Healing is the foundation upon which you can continue to build, with strength, clarity, and purpose.

Chapter 12: Support and Community Building

Burning the Script is an act of self-liberation, but it's also a collective act. You are not just reclaiming your own life, you are, in many ways, helping to build a new way of being for the world around you. And just as you need to heal, rest, and rebuild your energy, you also need to surround yourself with people who understand and support your journey. This transformation can be intense and emotionally challenging, and it's in the shared experiences and collective energy that we find the strength to continue.

Think about it: if you're going to burn the Script, why not do it with others who are also choosing to live authentically, to break free from the mould? It's not about going through this process alone; it's about walking this path with others who get it, who understand the ups and downs, the triumphs and setbacks. Having a community to turn to, people who are on a similar journey, gives you not just support, but also the accountability you need to keep going, even when it gets tough.

Start With Like-Minded Communities

The first step in building your support system is to find like-minded individuals who are also breaking free from their Scripts. This can be as simple as reaching out to friends, family, or colleagues who are open to transformation and self-growth or joining a local or online group focused on personal development, authenticity, or a specific area you're working to change.

There are many platforms where people are actively trying to burn their Scripts and build new, authentic lives. Look for online communities, Facebook groups, forums, or Instagram pages where people are sharing their struggles and victories. If you can't find a group that speaks to your specific needs, start one yourself. You don't have to wait for others to lead the way, you can be the one to create that space for connection.

You might find support in unexpected places: a co-worker, a neighbour, or a social media acquaintance might be silently struggling with their own Scripts and might be just waiting for someone to take the first step. Reach out, open up, and be vulnerable. Sharing your journey with others not only strengthens your commitment to your own transformation, but it encourages others to do the same.

Emotional Support: Finding Allies for the Journey

Building a community isn't just about finding people who are "like you" in a surface way, it's about finding people who understand your emotional journey. In many ways, burning the Script is a process of grieving and redefining yourself, and emotional support is key during these times.

Identify people in your life who can offer empathy and understanding, but that won't be enablers to allow you to stay stuck. These people will not try to fix you, but they will listen. They'll acknowledge the pain and the beauty of your transformation without judgment. These emotional allies are the ones who will cheer you on when you feel stuck, encourage you when you feel lost, and provide gentle accountability when you stray from the path.

You don't have to tell everyone in your life what you're going through, this is your personal journey, but you can create safe spaces where vulnerability is welcomed. Whether it's a close friend, a mentor, a therapist, or an online community member, the goal is to surround yourself with people who are supportive, empathetic, and aligned with your authentic self.

Emotional support isn't just about sympathy, it's about shared understanding and encouragement.

Accountability: Staying on Track

One of the most powerful aspects of community is accountability. It's easy to burn the Script in a moment of inspiration, but over time, the pressures of daily life can cause you to slip back into old habits. This is where having someone to keep you on track can be invaluable.

Accountability doesn't have to be about rigid rules or expectations. It's about creating a gentle system of check-ins that help you stay focused on your goals. Here's how you can do it:

1. **Partner Up:** Find an accountability partner, someone you trust who is also on a path of self-liberation. This could be a friend or someone in an online group you've connected with. Set regular check-ins (weekly or bi-weekly) where you discuss your progress, your challenges, and your intentions moving forward.
2. **Set Shared Goals:** In your community or with your accountability partner, establish small, tangible goals that you can work toward together. Whether it's setting boundaries with family members, making a career change, or simply

taking better care of yourself, having a goal makes the journey feel more concrete.

3. **Create Rituals:** One way to keep your transformation alive is to build shared rituals with your community. This could be a monthly virtual check-in where everyone shares their struggles and wins, or a group meditation practice to stay grounded. These rituals help you stay connected to your purpose and remind you that you are not alone.

4. **Celebrate the Small Wins:** Accountability also means recognizing progress, no matter how small. Celebrate the moments when you make a decision that aligns with your authentic self, whether it's saying no to something that no longer serves you, making a choice in line with your values, or simply showing up as your true self. Celebrate these moments with your community.

Building a Movement: Collective Liberation

This isn't just about one person burning their Script. This is about building a movement, a movement of individuals who are committed to shedding the old, oppressive narratives and stepping into the fullness of their authentic selves. When you join with others on this journey, you realize that the power of transformation is multiplied.

The more we connect with others who are also choosing liberation, the stronger our collective impact becomes. Each person who burns the Script is not just creating a new life for themselves, they are contributing to a larger societal shift, one that challenges outdated systems, expectations, and limitations. You're part of something bigger, something that can change the way we all live, relate, and show up in the world.

This is your invitation to step into that power, not alone, but together. Reach out, find your allies, and build your community. The journey is better when we walk it together.

Conclusion: The Fire is Yours to Keep

The Messy Middle is Where Most People Get Stuck

There arc plenty of people who start this work and never finish it. They read the all the books, listen to the speakers, attend the workshops, and get fired up about change, they become addicted to acquiring knowledge, until they hit the messy middle. The part where transformation is no longer just an idea, but a daily, uncomfortable reality.

And that's when the excuses come.

"That book didn't work for me."
"I tried, but nothing changed."
"Maybe this just isn't for me."

But the real question isn't whether this book or any other "worked." The question is: What work did you do with it?

Because let's be honest, this work is hard. It's messy. It's inconvenient. It forces you to look at parts of yourself and your life that you'd rather avoid. And that's why so many people get stuck. They hit the resistance, the discomfort, the pull to go back to what's easy, and they let it stop them.

But here's what I need you to know:

Your mess is your message.

The very thing that feels impossible right now, the fear, the uncertainty, the uncomfortable truth that won't leave you alone, is the thing that will become your superpower.

Your proof. Your trail YOU are blazing for those behind you.

Burning the Script Doesn't Have to Be a Life Revolution

I know my story might seem extreme, and scary. For me, burning the script meant coming out, ending a marriage, and tearing down a life that wasn't truly mine. It was a complete upheaval, messy, painful, and hard as hell.

But your path doesn't have to look like mine. There's no one-size-fits-all when it comes to rewriting your story. Reading this book won't force you into a massive life overhaul, unless that's what you choose. Burning the Script doesn't have to mean walking away from everything you know. It might just mean coming home to yourself.

Maybe for you, it's finally setting a boundary. Maybe it's changing careers, speaking your truth, or allowing yourself to want more. Maybe it's as small as acknowledging, just to yourself, that something in your life needs to change. There is no "right way" to do this work. The only requirement is that you don't stop when it gets hard.

The Truth About Freedom

Burning the Script is not a single act. It is a way of being. A way of choosing yourself, every single day, even when it feels impossible.

The world will try to pull you back. The voices of doubt, inside you and around you, will whisper that maybe you were safer in the Script, that maybe the life you left behind wasn't so bad, that maybe it's easier to just stay quiet. But you didn't come this far just to just come this far.

Freedom is not given. It is unlocked.

You unlock it every time you tell the truth instead of hiding behind what is expected.
You unlock it when you stop waiting for the "right" time and choose to start now.
You unlock it in the moments where you lean into discomfort instead of running back to what feels safe.
You unlock it when you trust that even if the next step is unknown, it is still yours to take.

This is what it means to Burn the Script, not just once, but over and over again, until there is nothing left standing but the truest, most unfiltered version of yourself.

A Life That is Yours

So, where do you go from here? That's the beautiful part, you get to decide.

There is no perfect roadmap, no step-by-step plan that guarantees a smooth path to self-liberation. There is only the fire you have already ignited inside yourself.

But I will leave you with this:

If you ever feel yourself slipping back into old patterns, remember - comfort is not the same as freedom. If you ever doubt your own power, remind yourself - no one is more qualified to shape your life than you. If you ever wonder whether it's worth it, ask yourself - what is the cost of staying where you are?

You did not come here to live a life of quiet discontent.
You did not come here to play small. You came here to be
fully alive. And if that means burning down everything
that was never truly yours, so be it.

The Fire is Yours

This book is ending. But your story is just beginning. The
question is no longer whether you will Burn the Script.
The question is: What will you create from the ashes?

Now go. Live unscripted.

www.ingramcontent.com/pod-product-compliance
Lightning Source LLC
Chambersburg PA
CBHW061752020426
42331CB00006B/1436